THE COLLECTOR'S ENCYCLOPEDIA OF

AKRO AGATE GLASSWARE

REVISED EDITION
FEATURING CURRENT VALUES

Gene Florence

COLLECTOR BOOKS
A Division of Schroeder Publishing

The current values in this book should be used only as a guide. They are not intended to set prices, which vary from one section of the country to another. Auction prices as well as dealer prices vary greatly and are affected by condition as well as demand. Neither the Author nor the Publisher assumes responsibility for any losses that might be incurred as a result of consulting this guide.

Searching For A Publisher?

We are always looking for knowledgeable people considered to be experts within their fields. If you feel that there is a real need for a book on your collectible subject and have a large comprehensive collection, contact us.

COLLECTOR BOOKS
P.O. Box 3009
Paducah, Kentucky 42002-3009

Additional copies of this book may be ordered from:

COLLECTOR BOOKS
P.O. Box 3009
Paducah, KY 42002-3009
or

May 1 – October 31	November 1 – April 30
Gene Florence	Gene Florence
P.O. Box 22186	Box 64
Lexington, KY 40522	Astatula, FL 34705

@ $14.95 Add $2.00 for postage and handling.

Copyright: Gene Florence, 1975
Values Updated 1992

This book or any part thereof may not be reproduced without the written consent of the Author and Publisher.
1 2 3 4 5 6 7 8 9 0

Printed by IMAGE GRAPHICS, INC., Paducah, Kentucky

OREWORD

As many of you know, I included Akro Agate as part of the second edition of *The Collectors Encyclopedia of Depression Glass.* Buying Akro for that book got me started searching for the children's pieces, but when I tried to find out about the larger pieces of Akro, I ran into all kinds of problems. First of all, there was no price guide to help me, and I found a wide range of prices on items among dealers and collectors. That's one reason for this book: there's a need for a price guide so that beginners and advanced collectors, too, can have an idea as to what values are asked. Also, there's a need for a relative guide to what is common and what is rare.

The information in the next few paragraphs is repeated throughout the main portions of the book, albeit not so concisely. I feel it is information that can bear repeating.

Since this may be the only book on Akro Agate you own, I should clearly state how you can identify this glassware. Unfortunately, there is no definite method of identification for all pieces. The easily identified pieces are the ones that bear the Akro symbol. This is a crow flying though the letter "A". The crow has a marble in its beak and one in each claw. This mark was used on the marble boxes in 1911 and then incorporated into the glassware around 1935. There may have been other marks tried by Akro as suggested in the section on ashtrays later in the book. However, it is doubtful that you will find another mark except the crow.

Many pieces only have "Made in U.S.A." on them, or you may find this along with a crow on some pieces. A very few pieces will have a mould number on them that identifies them as Akro. This is particularly true of the children's pieces. The most difficult thing to comprehend is that many pieces are not marked in any way.

In numerous places in this book, I will tell you what the piece will be numbered if it is marked. Akro used pattern numbers for many of their pieces; thus, if you will compare your piece to the description and number given here, you may be able to identify a questionable piece as being Akro. Still, numerous pieces will be identifiable only by the shapes and color characteristics of what you know is Akro.

What I have attempted to do is to whet your appetite as mine has been, so that even more discoveries of Akro can be unveiled in the future.

RICING

Prices are a reflection of what I have encountered over the twenty years I have been buying Akro Agate. Prices for most items are reasonable; certain colors of items are higher due to their being either scarce or more collectible. Prices for the extremely rare items are sometimes based on what has been offered for them, due to their not having been sold individually: often complete collections must be bought before one can lay hands on the genuinely rare item sought to begin with. Keep in mind that you are the one who determines price. If an item is priced too highly, then don't buy it, for when you do, you have set the price for the next customer.

EASUREMENTS

On large items, measurements are correct to within ¼ inch. Smaller items, such as children's pieces, are correct to within ⅛ inch. Mould variations do cause measurement fluctuations, so take this into consideration. Measurements are the perpendicular distance (right angle) from top rim to base on all items unless stated otherwise.

ABOUT the AUTHOR

Gene Florence, born in Lexington in 1944, graduated from the University of Kentucky where he held a double major in mathematics and English. He taught nine years in the Kentucky school systems at the Junior High and High School levels before his glass collecting "hobby" became his full time job.

Mr. Florence has been interested in "collecting" since childhood, beginning with baseball cards and progressing through comic books, coins, bottles and finally, glassware. He first became interested in Depression glassware after purchasing a set of Sharon dinnerware at a garage sale for $5.00. This interest in Depression glass led to his interest in Akro Agate.

He has written several books on glassware: *The Collector's Encyclopedia of Depression Glass*, now in its 10th edition, *The Collector's Encyclopedia of Akro Agate*, *The Collector's Encyclopedia of Occupied Japan* Volumes I, II, III, IV and V, *The Pocket Guide To Depression Glass*, now in its 7th edition, and *Kitchen Glassware of the Depression Years*, now in it's fourth edition.

Should you be in Lexington, he is often found at Grannie Bear Antique Shop, located at 120 Clay Avenue. This is the shop he helped his mother set up in what was formerly her children's day care center. The shop derived its name from the term of endearment the toddlers gave her.

Should you know of any unlisted or unusual pieces of glassware *in the patterns shown in this book*, you may write him at Box 22186, Lexington, KY 40522. If you expect a reply, you must enclose a self-addressed, stamped envelope and be patient. His travels and research often cause the hundreds of letters he receives weekly to backlog. He does appreciate your interest, however, and spends many hours answering your letters when time and circumstance permit.

ACKNOWLEDGMENTS

This book, first written eighteen years ago, and already reprinted twice, is literally back by popular demand! So many letters were received from collectors wanting not only updated pricing but the basic information that it was deemed necessary to reprint the book yet again to accommodate them.

However, even for a gung-ho publisher, I couldn't snatch pricing data overnight. In order to do justice to the book, I called on the expertise of some collectors and dealers whom I knew to be very current on Akro Agate pricing and information and who were willing to help in this enterprise.

A very special thanks is therefore due Larry Wells and Gladys Florence for their invaluable input — and to one other source who wishes to remain anonymous.

I'm very grateful for their informative, insightful comments regarding today's Akro market, which is thriving in spite of it's limited quantities. A thousand dollars may seem to novice collectors like an exorbitant price for an ash tray, yet several Akro brewery and soft drink advertising pieces have recently sold in the thousand dollar range. These same items were selling in the three hundred dollar price range a couple of years ago. Prices like these make Akro a viable collectible, and add incentive for serious collectors to take note of a field that they may have ignored until now!

The children's pieces, as always, are still much in demand. We all know that there is a strong market today for children's tea sets of every size, color and "species." There are fewer collectors for the utilitarian ware, yet many unusual colors and items in these lines are bringing premium prices today! As a collector, you can't afford to ignore Akro Agate wares. Happy Hunting!

CONTENTS

HISTORY

The history of Akro Agate has been traced in several other books via the memories of people involved. Because of this, there have been some erroneous dates that have crept into the Agate story. However, due to thorough research of court records and newspaper accounts by my friend, Glen Henley, I feel I can now accurately relate the rise and demise of the Akro Agate Company.

In 1911, The Akro Agate Company of Akron, Ohio, was established. The patent was applied for on March 23, 1911, and registered on August 22, 1911. Basically, the company was established to make marbles and games, which it continued to do until October 1, 1914, when the company moved to Clarksburg, West Virginia. The reasons for this move were mostly economic. Clarksburg offered cheap natural gas which was needed to heat the materials for making marbles, and the fine West Virginia sand for making glass marbles was readily available.

The Akro Agate Company prospered during World War I, when marbles were not imported from Germany. By the end of the war, Akro Agate had been able to produce marbles cheaply enough to beat the price of foreign imports and was able to establish itself as a major force in the marble industry. In fact, by the Depression, Akro Agate had about three-fourths of all the marble business of the United States.

Clinton Israel worked for Akro Agate from 1926 to 1930. He was able to improve the automatic marble making machine made by Horace C. Hill. Hill had patented his machine before the move to Clarksburg, but Clinton Israel's work was never patented. When questioned about the reasoning for this, he replied, "Then everyone would be able to make one by studying the patents." Because he did not patent his machine, many of the secrets of marble making remained with the marble producers.

In 1930, Israel was offered a position with a newly founded company, Master Marbles. For them, he was able to design similar machines.

This company began to eat into Akro Agate sales until they eventually were selling more marbles than Akro.

Thanks can be given to Master Marbles for Akro Agate glass, for it was because of them that the Akro Agate Company began to look in directions other than marbles. This is where the real story of Akro begins for many collectors.

In the middle 1930's, Akro began experimenting with a couple of new lines: a large, bulky ash tray and, in 1935 and 1936, children's dishes. To trace the beginning of these new lines, we must also look at a couple of other glass companies to see how they influenced or contributed to the change in Akro Agate products.

The Brilliant Glass Products Company, founded in Brilliant, Ohio, announced in the *Weston Independent* paper of June 15, 1927, that it was relocating to Weston, West Virginia. The reason for the move was that "Weston offers cheaper gas rates and better railway facilities than the former location." At the time, Brilliant manufactured colored glass products such as stop lights, stage flood lights, danger signal reflectors, bathroom fixtures and radio insulators.

In the October 26, 1927, issue of the *Weston Independent,* the Brilliant Glass Company announced an addition to the production line: "Westite," a marble-like glass which might be used for the production of bathroom fixtures, towel racks, etc. This form of glassware, named for the town, was patented by W. W. Mathews, superintendent of the plant.

Sometime between 1927 and 1936, Brilliant Glass Company adopted the name Westite from its major product's name. A 1933 catalogue reprint of Westite products is shown in the back of this book. This catalogue originally came from Mrs. John A. Henderson, whose husband was plant superintendent and general manager of Westite when the factory burned on July 16, 1936.

Westite's burning became a blessing for Akro Agate. All of the moulds, materials and other usable items from Westite were sold to Akro Agate. They got John Henderson to come to work for them and because of his experience with the Westite garden line products, such as flower pots and planters. Akro Agate emerged with a colorful line of Akro Agate flower pots and planters which caught on with the public. This line was indeed, their most important line until World War II, and bailed Akro Agate out of the declining marble business.

During World War II, the demand for metal for war materials along with the lack of imports of Japanese products allowed Akro Agate to control the market for doll dishes with their glass dishes which had not sold as well as metal dishes in the middle 1930's. Naturally, the metal "play" dishes had appealed to practical minded mamas more than glass ones had.

Instead of producing transparent colors and solid sets of green and pink, Akro Agate turned to mixed color sets and to the two-toned, commonly called marbleized, sets. These sets were produced and sold cheaply, and in 1942 and 1943, sales for Akro Agate products reached their peak. As the war ended, so did Akro Agate's prosperity. With the advent of imports, the returning use of metals, and the emergence of plastic, the death knell sounded. In 1951, the company was sold to the Clarksburg Glass Company, and the forty year history of Akro as it is known thus far came to an end.

• MARBLES •

The Akro Agate Company started with marbles, so it seems fitting we should start here also.

Akro Agate marbles are collectible today in many forms. Since so many Akro Agates were produced, there is not as great a demand for them singly by marble collectors as there is for some of the handmade, early marbles such as swirls and sulphides. Most collectors prefer agates in their original boxes as shown here because there are so many similar marbles without marks that this is a surer way of identifying them.

In the upper right of the picture is an Akro Solitary Checker game complete with instructions on how to win the game in your solitary hours.

At center back is a box of mixed size marbles containing the knee pad provided by the company so the player wouldn't wear his pants knees out — a selling pitch to Mom, no doubt. If worn, the pad is big enough to have saved a few knees and thus, perhaps, some rear ends.

A couple of older sets of boxed marbles are shown in the front. The center box is made of tin and depicts a game of marbles in progress. Around the box is the legend "Shoot Straight as a Kro* Flies," which accompanied many of the earlier boxed sets. The other box pictured I consider the most unique find. It consists of 100 marbles and 100 sticks of gum. A note inside the box says, "One stick of gum and one agate 1¢. Large agate free with last stick of gum purchased."

Considering that agates were made from 1911 at Akron, Ohio, up until the selling out in 1951 at Clarksburg, West Virginia, there must have been trillions of marbles scattered among the youngsters growing up in that forty-year period. Maybe you're a part of their history. Were you one of the ones around that circle with your favorite taw, playing "keeps?"

Pictured below the marbles are pieces of agate material which was disposed of at the Clarksburg site. Note the partial red-white teapot lid and the partial pumpkin colored cup with the Akro symbol embossed on it.

* "A KRO" was combined to make AKRO.

All prices given for marbles are for complete boxed sets in original condition.

Boxed set of 5	**$15.00**
Boxed set of 10	**$20.00**
** Boxed set of 25	**$35.00**
** Boxed set of 50	**$60.00**
Boxed set of 100	**$40.00**
Metal box set (early) (2 sizes)	**$40.00 – 75.00**
Cardinal red set (25)	**$100.00**
Solitary checker set	**$60.00**
Boxed set with original gum (100)	**$225.00**

** Chinese checker prices are slightly lower

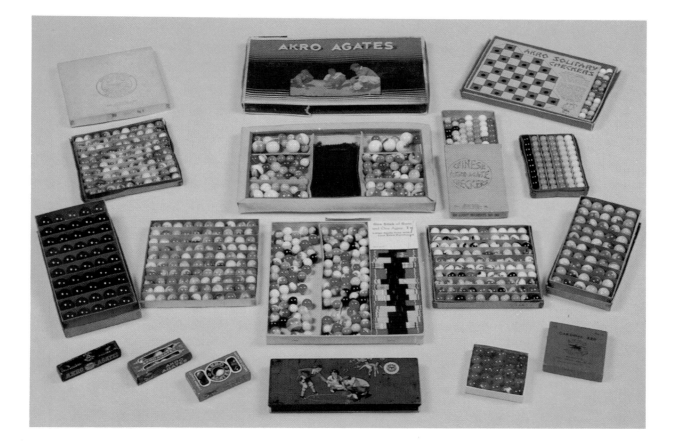

• WESTITE •

"Westite is distinctly American." So says a 1933 pamphlet reprinted in the back of this book. The story of Akro Agate could never be complete without an acknowledgement of the part this company played in its history, which is detailed in the section of history at the front of the book.

Akro bought the Westite moulds that remained after the Westite company burned in 1936. There is always some confusion about unmarked pieces in any form of glassware, but with Westite and Akro Agate, there is even some confusion on marked pieces as to whether they were made by Westite or by Akro Agate.

Westite came in several colors, but predominately it is found in a brown-white marbled color, a green, and a white-green. The red-white combination is not found as often and may be one of the colors used near the end of Westite's production. The pink tumblers are marked "Westite" and were undoubtedly made to sit on the bathroom or kitchen tumbler trays.

By carefully studying the Westite pieces, the Westite pamphlet, and the Akro Agate pieces of several collections, the following conclusions have been drawn: Westite pieces are sometimes marked, but more often they are not. The pieces of Westite are usually found in colors not used by Akro Agate. Akro Agate used Westite moulds which they obtained after the Westite factory burned, but the items produced from these moulds were, naturally, in colors typical of Akro. Later, some of these same mould productions added the Akro trademark symbol, the crow, and production was continued. Therefore, it is possible to find an umarked piece in a Westite shape that is Akro.

The confusing thing to this whole business is a symbol on some pieces of typically colored Akro. These items are marked with a "W" inside a diamond shape, ⬦. There is speculation that these items were not Westite due to the colors found. Another version is that these items were made for Woolworth's, which was one of Akro's biggest customers. This last seems a little far-fetched in that other items known to be those made for Woolworth's bear no such mark. Taking all possibilities into consideration, I believe this could be a form of Westite mark carried on at Akro Agate and later removed.

The Brilliant Glass Company's influence can be seen in the bathroom and kitchen fixtures shown here. It is no wonder that the use of these was limited, as they chip and break quite easily.

The large footed bowl in rear left found its way late into Akro's line. The ivy bowl was also sold with a lid as shown in left front. This carries an embossed "Ramses" on its base.

No attempt will be made here to price Westite. I consider it to be much more rare than Akro Agate although not as colorful. Only time will tell as to its collectibility.

• ASH TRAYS •

The large, heavy looking ash trays at back are thought to be the first items Akro Agate made when switching from making marbles exclusively. As you can see, they expanded over the years to include various shapes and a multitude of colors. You can see the basic shapes and colors, so let's talk about what is hard to find and what is common.

The shell (marking 246) and leaf (marking 245) are common although many people don't even realize these are Akro Agate. Although these are multitudinous, you might look for color combinations that are unusual.

The small square ash trays (marking 252) came either separate or as a set including the cigarette or match holders shown in the back row. The smoker set was boxed with the match holder and four matching ashtrays. This set, alone, shows a sample of the colors available since there is a pumpkin color and a black amethyst stacked under the yellow. In case you are not familiar with black amethyst, it's a color that looks black until it's held up to the light, where it shows purple.

The next most common ash tray is the rectangular with the cigarette tabs at the ends (marking 249). The color combinations in this are usually more vivid than the other types.

The heavy hexagonal ash trays pictured are not very common. The crystal, transparent brown and the satin finish "lemonade and oxblood" (yellow and red) would be the most difficult colors to find them in. Crystal Akro Agate pieces are extremely rare in anything save bells, so keep that in mind. You can even see that ol' crow on the crystal one pictured here. I'd like to point out that the ash tray you see in the left back is a factory mistake, but it has the crow trademark also.

The other style of ash tray is left of center at the back of the picture. These are rounded with slashed tabs to hold cigarettes. These are the most difficult ash trays to find save for the solid blue with the straight out tab. The latter is the rarest of all the ash tray styles shown here, so look for it.

+ shows measurements that include the tabs

	SOLID COLORS	MARBLEIZED
Leaf	----------	$4.50 *
Shell	----------	$4.00 *
3" Square	$3.00 **	$5.00
4½" Hexagonal+	----------	$15.00 ***
5" Ellipsoid+	----------	$18.00
4" Rectangular	----------	$5.00
4½"	$40.00	----------
5¼" Square (heavy)	$60.00 ****	$40.00
3" Match Holder	$10.00	$7.50

* Double for very colorful

** Black – $20.00; pumpkin – $12.50

*** Crystal – $40.00; amber – $65.00; lemonade and oxblood – $100.00

**** Black – $75.00

• BELLS, BASKETS AND MISCELLANEOUS •

The mould for the bell has been used by other companies, yet there is an easy method for making sure your bell is Akro. Turn it so that you can see inside near the attached clanger. Where the bell meets the handle, you should see a "made in U.S.A ." mark, if it isn't hidden by the clanger. On many you can even see that crow flying. Bells, particularly Agate ones, are very good Akro items to own! I wish you lots o' luck finding them.

All the bells here are marked, including the crystal one. A friend has a crystal bell which serves as a dome for a bottle of perfume resting on a satin pillow. I'm sorry we didn't get it photographed.

Bennet's reproduced bells should have a "B" on them which clearly marks them as newer. You will find the "B" in the same place as Akro Agate's mark.

The two-handled basket (pattern 328, though you won't find it marked) has been made by the Smith Glass Company in all colors for years. In fact, I sometimes wonder if Akro didn't maybe borrow moulds from other glass companies for some of their wares. This practice was not all that uncommon, as has been vouched for by numerous workers at glass plants from the Depression era.

The green-white, blue-white, orange-white, and solid white seem to be the only colors that Akro Agate produced. Any others,

unless typical of Akro coloration, would have to be labeled as belonging to another company, probably Smith.

The basket with only one handle is the one of extreme importance to collectors of Akro. It's the item they have "heart failure" over, so to speak. I can confirm the actual existence of eleven, which are green-white or orange-white marbleized. These one-handled baskets were tried as a special promotion for Easter, but if the cooling process didn't snap the handles, then handling them did. So, as far as can be determined, they were never sold; they exist only because some factory workers took them home. If you stumble onto one of these, then you've found something!

The little bowl in the forefront is a finger bowl, but unmarked.

Three sugars, yellow, white, and pink, and one creamer in pink are all that have surfaced so far. The pink is similar to Crown Tuscan pink and tends to stimulate argument until turned over and the little crow kind of winks at the disbeliever.

That odd shaped flower pot was brought to the photography studio on the first day and caused quite a little discussion, but it's clearly marked. Maybe you have one! It's marked 1308, stands 6½" high and is 6¹⁵⁄₁₆" wide.

	SOLID COLORS	PUMPKIN	MARBLEIZED
* Bell, 5¼" tall	$60.00	100.00	----------
Basket, 2 handles	$15.00	----------	$27.50
** Basket, 1 handle	----------	----------	$250.00
Creamer, 3"	$225.00	----------	----------
Sugar, 3"	$225.00	----------	----------
Bowl, finger	----------	----------	$10.00
6½" flower pot	$65.00	$75.00	----------

* Crystal – $20.00; white – $50.00; yellow – $90.00
  Add $30.00 – 50.00 if perfume bottle still in bell.

** Blue-white – $295.00

• BOWLS AND CANDLESTICKS •

The tab-handled bowl looking like it has ears is marked 321; it was sold separately and with candlesticks to match. Akro made several styles of candlesticks, but these are the only ones I can identify. There are shorter candlesticks that are quite colorful being passed off as Akro with "No. 851" written on the base. Akro never used the word *number* or its abbreviation on their pieces, however.

The three-footed bowl (flared at top with darts inside) in orange-white marbleized, the green, and the pumpkin, are marked 340. The plain blue bowl at right rear is marked 323. This particular item was later encircled with an ivy design and covered, thereby creating a powder jar.

The stacked bowls in the back are marked 320; however, you will find both plain and ruffled tops as is the case of the stacked bowls near left center.

The plain white bowl shown is possibly Westite and as such would be a forerunner of Akro bowls. The plain "Stacked Disc" bowl was probably a Woolworth's cereal bowl, but it has no marked number, just a crow trademark.

Of interest to collectors are the large, footed fruit bowls which are quite rare. Notice the rather typical Akro rim which matches the design on the smaller bowls. Cobalt blue, black and pumpkin are the only colors in which I have seen these, but you might find others.

	SOLID COLORS	COBALT/ PUMPKIN	MARBLEIZED
7¼" tab handled (9" with tabs)	$22.50	$32.50	$30.00
6" diameter, 3 footed	$18.00	$27.50	$25.00
5¼" diameter, 3 footed (darts or ribs & flutes)	$20.00	$20.00	$27.50
5¼" stacked disc	$25.00	----------	----------
candlesticks, 3¼", pr.	$100.00	$125.00	$150.00
* 6" tall, 8" diameter, footed	$100.00	$125.00	$150.00

* Black amethyst – $200.00

• DEMITASSE CUP AND SAUCER SETS •

Since the children's marbleized pieces were made in the late 1930's, it can be safely assumed that these sets in the marbleized colors were from that same era.

There are two shades of each of the green-blue combinations. Both can be found with white and with a creme colored background. The orange-white seems to be the easiest to find. The solid green was made from the same mould as the marbleized and it is close in color to some pieces of Chiquita children's dishes I've seen. All of these marbleized sets differ from the solid

sets in the picture in two ways: the cups are shorter by ¼" and the saucers lie flatter and are approximately ⅜" smaller in diameter.

The other solid color demitasse cups and saucers occur in the colors shown plus some others. I have no yellow saucer for my cup, and I annihilated the beige saucer all by myself. Our concrete garage floor is hard on dropped glass.

Many of these will have only a "made in U.S.A." marking with a mold number on them. Many collectors of demitasse cups and saucers do not know these items are Akro.

* Marbleized sets	cup 2⅛", saucer 4¼"	**$12.50**
Solid color set (except green)	cup 2⅜", saucer 4⅝"	**$8.00**
Solid green set	cup 2⅜", saucer 4⅝"	**$5.00**

* Blue-white marbleized – $15.00

• FLOWER POTS (GRADUATED DARTS) •

"Graduated Darts" flower pots come in varied sizes, from the dainty little 2" pots with their individual water saucers to the granddaddy 7" size. The 2" pots come with and without a drilled hole and matching underplates. Each of the 2" pots has 5 darts, while the 2½" have 3 darts.

In front of the "granddaddy" pot is pictured the 3" size in a light pink with a light green swirl. This size comes with either a straight or scalloped top, as do the 4" pots. A pumpkin, scalloped top one, unfortunately,

got left in Ohio at photography time. For the sake of variety, a hand fluted pot with six flutations and two with fired on decorations are also pictured in the 4" size. This decorating process must have come over from Westite as you can see samples of this in the Westite catalogue reprinted at the back of this book.

The next size varies from 5¼" to 5½" and is represented by the fluted pots shown. One of these carries 5 flutes, the other 6. There aren't many of these.

	SOLID COLORS	COBALT/ PUMPKIN	MARBLEIZED
* 2" without saucer	$5.00	$12.00	$5.00
2½"	$5.00	$12.00	$5.00
3" smooth top	$5.00	$7.50	$5.00
3" scalloped top	$7.00	$10.00	$6.00
** 4" smooth top	$6.00	$10.00	$6.00
4" scalloped top	$8.00	$13.50	$7.00
*** 5¼"	$15.00 ****	$22.50	$15.00
7"	$85.00	$100.00	$25.00

* Saucer only – $15.00

** Decorated – $17.50; fluted $55.00

*** Hand fluted – $65.00

**** Black amethyst – $50.00; fluted – $75.00

• FLOWER POTS (RIBBED TOPS) •

There are seven sizes of these pots shown which range in practically every color imaginable. The smallest size is 1¼" tall, but it was listed as 1 inch by Akro; the largest is 4 inches tall. There are several notable points to ponder about this style of flower pot. First of all, the wire racks were designed especially for the flower pots, but probably not by Akro. Many companies sold their wares in quantity to another manufacturer who made metal stands, or whatever, for the glassware purchased. This would ac-count for these stands not having been made at Clarksburg.

In the lower right, the darker green pot (above the blue-white) and the gray-green pot on the bottom of the stack of three are marked "Braun & Corwin."

You will find the black amethyst ribbed top flower pot fairly difficult to find. My favorite, however, (if you can really say I have a favorite flower pot) is the 4 inch "Spatterglass," blue-white (back, right of center.)

The following sizes are shown:

1¼", (290, though probably will not find this one marked.)
1¾", (291, though probably will not find this one marked.)
2¼", marked 291½
2⅜", (292, though probably will not find this one marked.)
2⅝", marked 300F
3½", marked 293
4", marked 294

	SOLID COLORS*	COBALT/ PUMPKIN	MARBLEIZED
1¼"	$9.00	$15.00	$12.00
1¾"	$3.00	$4.00	$3.00
2¼"	$3.00	$4.00	$3.00
2⅜"	$3.50	$7.00	$4.00
2⅝"	$3.50	$7.00	$4.00
3½"	$5.00	$8.00	$5.00
4"	$7.50	$12.50	$8.00
4" stand	$35.00	$40.00	$40.00

* Triple price for black amethyst

Wire holders $5.00 – $10.00

• FLOWER POTS (RIBS AND FLUTES) •

The "Ribs and Flutes" style has the same design on the sides. Yet, some of the top edges are smooth while others are irregularly scalloped. Where the flutes go to the top, there is a wide scallop, but where there is a rib there is a narrow scallop. The same number marking is used whether the top is scalloped or plain.

The specially made flower pot in the lower left took a special hand tool to do, and the six flutings were made while the agate was still hot. Many of these cracked while cooling, which may account for not too many being around today.

The 5½" tall, large sized blue pot at right rear has factory applied, hand painted flowers. These are fired on under the glaze. Few have surfaced. The wire holders prove interesting, especially the one with the Akro base which is mostly hidden. The blue base matches the two blue pots enclosed in the holders. You will find 9 ribs and 9 flutes on each of these regardless of size. The following sizes are shown:

3" smooth or scalloped top, mark 297
3½" smooth or scalloped top, mark 296
3¾" smooth or scalloped top, mark 305
5½" smooth or scalloped top, mark 307

	SOLID COLORS	COBALT/ PUMPKIN	MARBLEIZED
3" smooth top	$4.50	$7.50	$5.00
3" scalloped top	$3.50	$7.50	$4.00
3½" smooth top	$4.00	$7.50	$4.50
3½" scalloped top	$4.00	$7.50	$4.50
* 3¾" smooth top	$6.00	$8.00	$6.00
3¼" scalloped top	$6.00	$8.00	$6.00
**5½" smooth top	$15.00	$20.00	$17.50
5½" scalloped top	$15.00	$20.00	$17.50

* Fluted – $50.00

**Fluted – $65.00

• FLOWER POTS (STACKED DISC AND BANDED DART) •

"Stacked Disc" and "Banded Dart" are the two patterns shown here. You will recognize "Stacked Disc" by its name. "Banded Dart" has a row of darts around the top edge and four groups of three below the banded edge of the pot. There are four sizes of "Stacked Disc," but I have only found three in the "Banded Dart."

The sizes of "Stacked Disc" are as follows:

2½", 5 discs
3", 6 discs
4", 8 discs
5½", 8 discs

The size in which "Banded Dart" is found are:

2½" marked 300
3¼" no mark
5½" no mark

You might note that the "Stacked Disc" comes only in marbleized colors whereas the "Banded Dart" comes in both marbleized and solid colors. The black amethyst, though, will take a lot of searching. Cobalt blue and pumpkin are collector's favorites.

The "Banded Dart" pots are the only Akro pots that have a ribbed interior. Four ribs run inside the pot, similar to Westite, so it is possible to conclude that these were early conversions of Westite moulds. This might account for the scarcity of "Banded Dart" flower pots.

The 6 disc, 3" tall flower pot seems to be the most difficult size of "Stacked Disc," but the largest size of "Banded Dart" is hardest to find.

Flower Pots (Stacked Disc)

	MARBLEIZED ONLY *
2½"	$3.50
3"	$6.00
4"	$7.50
5½"	$15.00

*Exceptionally colorful flower pots will bring up to double prices shown.

Flower pots (Banded Dart)

	SOLID COLORS	COBALT/ PUMPKIN	MARBLEIZED
2½"	*$15.00	$20.00	$15.00
3¼"	$20.00	$25.00	$20.00
5½"	$30.00	$35.00	$30.00

*Black amethyst – $35.00

• JARDINIERES •

The five styles shown are colorful, *n'est-ce pas?*

The square mouth type shown at the back has three styles. The scalloped tip comes in the "Graduated Darts" and the "Ribs and Flutes" patterns. The latter style, shown in green and green-white, is marked 306 and has the flying crow symbol.

The smooth top, square jardinieres shown have two distinct markings. The green-white and the cobalt blue are marked Akro Agate, 306. The pumpkin and green are marked with a "W" enclosed in a diamond. As discussed under the section on Westite, it's not known whether this is a Westite marking or a mark used by Akro Agate to mark their good customer "Woolworth" products. The colors here are typical of those on Akro. I prefer my speculation to the latter one. It seems likely, since it's an Akro color, that Akro made it from the Westite moulds they purchased; later on, since you can find ones without this W marking, they just removed the marking of the other company. I freely admit to speculation here and welcome any factual rendition from readers!

The tab-eared, rectangular jardiniere with 7 darts is the most bountiful, but even it is not as plentiful as many of the flower pots. Be sure to check tab handles when buying, as they damaged easily! Cracks and chips abound. Cobalt blue and pumpkin colors remain collector's delights as is true in most Akro Agate items. Notice that even the so-called solid colors have shadings of color.

The bell shaped, rectangular jardiniere shown at front in cobalt blue is the most difficult shape to come by. It is found with 8 darts and is desirable in any color.

	SOLID COLORS	COBALT/ PUMPKIN	MARBLEIZED
5", graduated darts, smooth top	$15.00	$25.00	$13.00
5", grad. dart, scalloped	$15.00	$25.00	$15.00
5", ribs & flutes, sq. top	$17.50	$25.00	$15.00
4½" rectangular top	$20.00	$30.00	$15.00
4¾" bell shaped, rect. top	$20.00	$25.00	$20.00

• LAMPS •

Akro made numerous lamps and lamp parts. None that I have ever heard about were marked, so the only way to recognize one is to know Akro characteristics, i.e., colors and shapes.

The picture contains representative pieces of the odd color combination plus it shows the shapes of the lamps made. The parts shown were found at the factory site. There were a lot of other parts, but these were the larger ones.

The hanging wall lamp is found with a shade similar to the one on the center lamp. Most of the lamps you see will be of the off white hue with orange or brownish swirls; don't, however, overlook other obvious combinations such as blue-white. That particular error took me back three times to a shop in Ohio last summer, never to find it open. That wouldn't be so bad had I not driven over a hundred miles out of the way each time!

One bothersome point to some is that cords are usually in very poor shape on these lamps. Now, if my sister can demonstrate how to re-wire a lamp to her college class, it's got to be a simple process! So don't allow a little matter of cord replacement to stand in your way. It takes only a few minutes to re-wire these lamps since they come apart very easily. It's safer to use new wire than that made 40 or so years ago anyway.

Note: We now know lamp with black base on left and blue and white lamp on right are not Akro.

Lamps without Akro shade   **$50.00**
Lamps with Akro shade   **$175.00**
Hanging Wall lamps with shade   **$150.00**
Hanging Wall lamp without shade   **$35.00**

• POWDER JARS •

Shown here is the most desirable of all the Akro Agate single pieces, the "apple" puff box (pattern 806, if marked). The pumpkin colored apple shown represents the most common color of the few known. On the right is an orange and creme top on a crystal bottom. The crystal apples here are of recent origin, so look for only the Agate ones. The top on the crystal base was dug up at the plant site by an Akro enthusiast. The digger said he dug a hole that was "headed for China" trying to find the bottom to go with it, but alas, he had no success.

The jars with the sombrero top are called Mexicali jars from the name on them. The Pick Wick Cosmetic firm of New York distributed these cigarette jars as containers for their spice bath powder. Notice the topless blue-white jar in front with the hats off to the side. A yellow, probably experimental, hat is turned over to show the inside. The reason I feel it experimental is because the hat does not have a ridge to hold it on top the jar as do normal sombreros.

The ivy embossed covered jars (pattern 323), as well as the other two bowls, are examples of an Akro habit of using one mould to serve two purposes. By making a lid for the bowl, they achieved a powder jar. They must have employed somebody full time to just study old moulds to see what new thing could be made.

The other two powder jars pictured come in a variety of colors, but they have no pattern numbers to use as guides. The swirled marble effect which is typical of Akro is easily seen, but you might find some of these in colors other than those Akro used, so be wary of them. The ribbed jars seem safe enough to buy in the above colors, plus a shade of blue similar to the background in the picture.

The three-legged jar with the gradually increasing rings doesn't seem to pop up in any colors other than those known to be Akro, so this should not be a problem. I guess we had better call this one "Concentric Ring" to go with an Akro name.

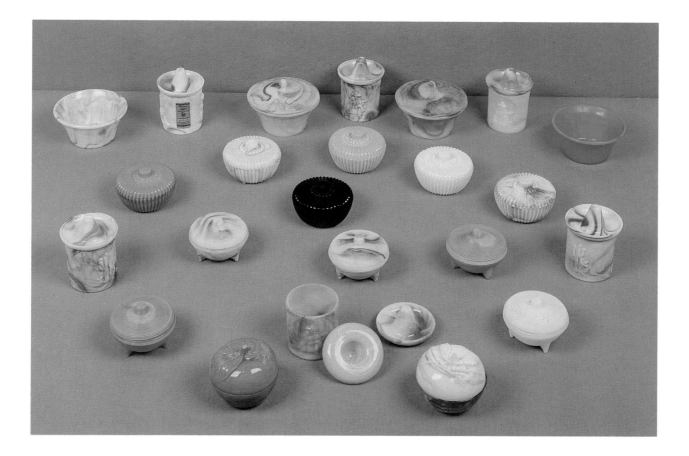

	SOLID COLORS	MARBLEIZED
* Apple	$225.00	$275.00
Concentric Ring Powder Jar,		
3 footed	$20.00	$30.00
Ivy Powder Jar & Cover	----------	$40.00
Ivy Bowl, no cover	$7.50	$10.00
Mexicali with hat	----------	$30.00 **
Ribbed	$10.00 ***	$27.50

  * Crystal without notch – $100.00

  ** Blue-white – $35.00; green-white – $30.00

*** Black – $30.00

    Blue – $20.00

    Yellow – $18.00

• PLANTERS •

Here are three styles of planters: two are rectangular in shape, the other eight sided planter is large, irregularly shaped and practically unknown to Akro collectors due to its scarcity.

You will find rectangular planters relatively easy to locate except for the fired-on, decorated blue in front. All decorated Akro is quite rare.

The holders for the rectangular planters are quite unusual. The little wagon and the ivy leaves show plainly. I would have liked to have shown the little donkey with his two bundles which are planters.

The smaller, rectangular planter from pattern 656 is 6" long. The 8" rectangular is a product of pattern 653. You will need to search for the unusual colors or try to locate marbleized pieces in the larger rectangular planter if you're interested in the more collectible pieces. They should exist though I haven't found any yet. If you're just planting flowers, then latch onto whatever you like.

The larger, irregularly shaped planter measures 11½" x 7" and is rather heavy. The darts on it are in even numbers whereas the other Akro pieces have odd numbered darts. Specifically, there are sixteen darts across the larger center piece and eight on each of the smaller sections. To verify this, all you have to do is find one!

The three other styles of planters shown in the lower photograph are plentiful only in the 6" oval size, marked 654. The large, 8½" long by 4⅜" planter is marked 651, but I have only seen one of these marked. You can see 7 darts on each of these except the white, which is plain. The white is probably earlier and is possibly Westite.

Candlesticks came with these large planters as well as with the tab-handled bowls shown on page 16. The pumpkin candlesticks pictured are the only pair I've ever seen in that color. You might find them in any color here; cobalt blue ones would be nice! The large sized bowls seem to be found only in the solid Agate colors. I won't be too amazed if someone discovers a marbleized planter.

The rounded rectangular planter isn't found in large quantities, so you might keep your eyes open for these in both solid and marbleized colors. Look, too, for the decorated oval dishes, as this one is the first I've seen. I hope someone finds a warehouse filled with decorated Akro items. There are just too few of these to be found with the original factory fired-on decorations!

The wire holders had to be specially made to fit the oval dishes of Akro; it's important to note that you will find these oval dishes sans the Akro trademark and in colors not typical of Akro. These were made later at Clarksburg by the Clarksburg Glass Co. using Akro moulds with the trademark removed.

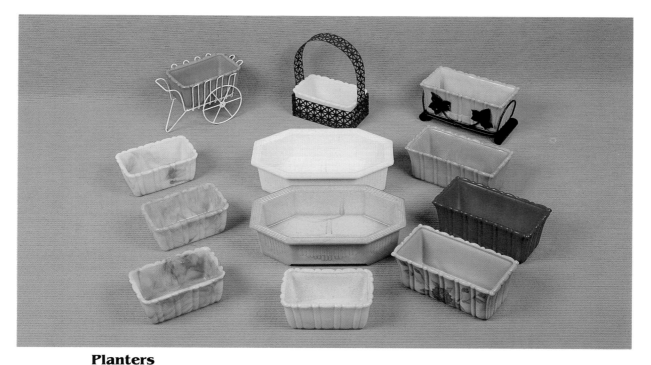

Planters

	SOLID COLORS	PUMPKIN	MARBLEIZED
11½" x 7", irreg. shape	$100.00	$125.00	----------
* 8" rectangular	$10.00	$22.00	----------
6" rectangular	$4.00	$10.00	$4.00

* Factory decorated – $35.00

Planters (oval)

	SOLID COLORS	PUMPKIN	MARBLEIZED
* 6" oval	$3.50	$7.50	$5.00
8" rounded rectangular	$13.00	$25.00	$10.00
8½" x 4⅜"	$20.00	$27.50	$20.00
candlestick, 3¼", pr.	$100.00	$125.00	$150.00

* Factory decorated – $32.50

• COLONIAL LADY PUFF BOX, 1939 – 1942 •
• SCOTTY DOG PUFF BOX, 1939 – 1942 •

One of the most familiar items to non-collectors of Akro Agate are the Colonial Lady and Scotty Dog puff boxes. Commonly called powder jars, these items were listed as puff boxes by Akro Agate.

Evidence in the form of a 29¢ price tag from J.J. Newberry located inside the top of the cobalt blue Colonial Lady rules out speculation that these items were a giveaway item for a cosmetic firm. They were made for the dime store trade and, as pointed out earlier, Woolworth's was one of Akro Agate's biggest customers.

Finding Scotty Dogs with perfect ears gets to be quite a job, as they were easily damaged. Note the dark green one without a base as a prime example of "one earedness." This top was included to show the color and since it was dug up, you can see the soil's action upon the glass. You can see how the base looks by itself in the foreground.

Notice the indentations around the bases of both the Colonial Lady and the Scotty Dog. This has led more than one person to conclude that the puff boxes were made at different times with one being re-designed from the other. However, both were made for a period of four years between 1939 and

1942. The Colonial Lady will be more common than the Scotty due to the aforementioned breakage factor and also due to the fact that the Colonial Lady was a little more popular and more were made.

The white and pink puff boxes will be easiest to find. The Colonial Lady is shown in five shades of blue, but you will have to search many a day to duplicate these. Most difficult of the blues would be the cobalt located in the center and the ice blue to its left. Rather than try to name each of the blues shown here, I will assure you that the other three are all equally available, just not as plentiful as the white or pink. The green will be about as difficult to find as the cobalt, but the two-toned green and white may well be unique. I have heard of no other, so if you have one, please let me know!

The Scotty Dogs follow the same pattern of difficulty with the blues following the pink and white in abundance. The green is probably the next most difficult with the transparent amber and crystal nearly impossible to find.

As previously pointed out, the crystal Akro is undoubtedly the rarest color in all items except the bells.

	COLONIAL LADY MOLD NO. 647	SCOTTY DOG MOLD NO. 649
White, Pink	$50.00	$60.00
Blue (several shades)	$60.00	$75.00
Cobalt, Ice Blue	$225.00	$250.00
Lime Green	$175.00	225.00
Dark Green	----------	$150.00
Transparent Colors	$325.00	$325.00

* Two-tone with white – $300.00

• SMALL URNS AND VASES •

This photo shows four styles of small souvenir items that Akro made as well as a couple of other advertising pieces. The cornucopias (marked 765) are probably the most often found of the four. You can see a couple of differences in the ones shown if you look closely at the base. Those in the front on the left all have a raised tip whereas the others in the picture have a rounded, turned down point. These were made from 1941 to 1943. The Guernsey Glass Company now owns this mould, and if unusual, non-Akro colors are spotted, look for a "B" on the inside bottom. This stands for Harold Bennett's name. He was president of the Guernsey Glass Company. Also, you may find an (IG) mark on the base of some that are made by the Imperial Glass Company. The only sure way to identify Akro is by its known colors or the pattern number 765 on the base.

The small urns or vases with a square foot and beaded top (lined across the back) were made for a company in New York. The base of some of these, as well as some of the cornucopias, is embossed "N.Y.C. Vogue Merc. Co., U.S.A." Many of these pieces, as do some of the other vases of other styles, have paper stickers on them which say "Souvenir of West Virginia," or "New York," or even "Arcadia, New York."

The vase with a six-sided foot and serrated top is found in a variety of colors; notice in particular the one on the left which tries to be a good imitation of lemonade and oxblood — a color found usually in children's pieces. This vase, pattern 764, was made from 1941 through 1943.

The most difficult of the small vases to find is the hand shaped one, pattern 766, made also from 1941 to 1943. It's rarely found in mint condition due to its thinness. Of the six pictured, only two are mint. When I've run into these in antique shops, flea markets, etc., they have usually had fairly high prices and the usual damage. I have never been lucky enough to find a perfect one outside a collection.

Cornucopias, 3¼"   **$2.00 – $8.00 for very colorful**
Urn with square foot, 3¼"   **$3.00 plain – $10.00 very colorful**
Vase with six sided foot, 3¼"   **$4.00 plain – $12.00 very colorful**
Vase in shape of hand, 3¼"   **$7.50 plain – $17.50 very colorful**

• TALL VASES •

Akro Agate vases are numerous and colorful. This picture shows early pieces as well as the traditional pieces made from the Westite moulds. The tall, 8¾" brown and white vase in the rear is most definitely Westite before they ever started using the "Graduated Darts" on their vases.

The remaining vases of the 8¾" size are marked Akro Agate and carry the odd numbered darts, seven in this case, so typical of Akro pieces. The three vases with scalloped tops shown in the center fit the pattern "Ribs and Flutes" and will be seen throughout the wares made for ornamental and decorative purposes. These always seem to occur in nine ribs and nine flutes. The smaller "brothers" of these, shown to the right and left in green-white and pumpkin colors, have scalloped tops, but they have seven darts instead of ribs and flutes.

The idea for the little stands with rounded corners seating some vases in the picture came from Westite, as can be seen in the green-white square shaped one in the front, yet these are marked

Akro Agate and are found with these styles of vases and some flower pots.

The vase on the stand is likely Westite. Notice its plainness as opposed to the five others of varying colors which have six of the darts running from the top edge downward. These vases all stand 6¼" tall. The most striking is the marbled orange-white in front which has been fluted seven times. These fluted Akro Agate pieces are hard to find, so watch for them. The fluting had to be done by hand. Since there seem to be so few of these, this fluting may have proven too time consuming, or perhaps it wasn't accepted by consumers. The tool specially designed for doing this fluting was at Evansville when we photographed; however, it doesn't seem to have gotten photographed! Sorry.

The white, 6¼" vase in the foreground has a larger foot protruding on each side and a smooth top compared to the 6¼" ruffled top vases with three small feet. The heavy, three-footed vase is very difficult to find.

	SOLID COLORS	COBALT/ PUMPKIN	MARBLEIZED
8¾", 7 darts	$30.00	$60.00	$35.00
8" ribs and flutes	$100.00	$125.00	$125.00
* 6¼" tab handles	$35.00	$50.00	$40.00
6¼" scalloped top	$50.00	$60.00	$60.00
6¼" smooth top	$65.00	----------	----------
Stand, 4"	$30.00	$35.00	$35.00

* Hand fluted – $85.00

• JEAN VIVAUDOU CO., INC. & RELATED ITEMS •

Another of Akro's customers was the Jean Vivaudou Company, Inc., of New York. They bought Akro products to sell their cosmetic products in and this became a boon for both companies. The white items which were supposed to look like milk glass became a standard item for the J.V. Company. You will find a "J.V. Co., Inc." embossed on each of these pieces. The white is the most common, followed by pink, black and the powder blue which remains most elusive. Very few people have seen the powder blue; it must have been used sparingly, or the product cost more, or turned more people "off" than "on." The possibilities are endless.

The tops to the shaving mugs slip off easily, and if that doesn't happen, then the fact that the knobs break off quite readily could leave you with an unlidded mug. Unfortunately, the black one pictured did not survive the trip back to Lexington after the photography session in Evansville.

The decorated powder jars are attractive. Since the blue top in the center was very close to the color of the background, it was placed on the white powder jar to show the contrast. This color blue may be difficult to find, but be aware of its existence while out searching for these treasures.

The bottom picture is included here because the flower vases in the back row were used by the J.V. Company to package their sachet products. To quote from a label from one of these vases, "Orloff Sachet Flower Vase — with exclusive Orloff Bouquet/ Parfums Orloff Made in U.S.A. No. 304." The pattern number on this vase is 658. I might also point out that the black vase in the rear center is new. Notice the round base instead of oval as well as its having holes drilled into each side of the base for mounting. These were made since 1970 but cause no problem in identification.

The rectangular garden dish, marked 657, used the same basic design as the vase above. You will find that both of these items are quite plentiful, so look for the prettier colors. You can be choosey if you know that an item is plentiful.

The little urn or vase has an embossed flower. This piece will not be easily found and when it is, it must be examined closely since the little tab handle and the base are delicate and thin.

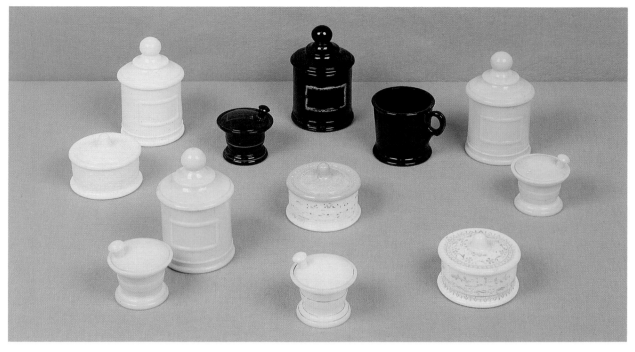

	WHITE	PINK	BLACK	BLUE
Apothecary jar	$15.00	$65.00	$50.00	$65.00
Shaving mug (mortar & pestle)	$10.00	$25.00	$25.00	$25.00
Mug		----------	$30.00	----------
Powder Box	$20.00 *	$65.00	----------	$100.00 (darker blue)

*Decorated – $30.00 (add $10.00 – 20.00 if contents intact)

	SOLID	MARBLEIZED
Planter, rectangular	$4.00	$4.00
Vase, embossed flowers	$4.00	$5.50
Urn, tab handles, 3¼"	$10.00	$15.00

• ADVERTISING ASH TRAYS & MISC. AKRO •

*The most interesting item pictured is the cigarette tray match holder (pattern 805.) This was made for the Hamilton Match Company of Cincinnati, Ohio. The same item, sans matches or stand to hold them, is pictured next to it in transparent brown.

Most noticeable are the Goodrich Tires which were used as ash trays (pattern 251) or for ball point pen holders (pattern 250).

The pumpkin and green ash trays with the match book holders in the center were made for the Hotel Lincoln in New York; the blue was made for the Hotel Edison in New York.

The rectangular ash tray to the left has the words "Akro Agate Ware" embossed on the inside, leading one to believe it was an advertising piece for themselves.

The small, green, oval, satin finished pieces of glass says, "Heinz 57 Varieties." The only way to link this to Akro Agate except via records is that it was dug up by an Akro enthusiast at the Akro plant site in Clarksburg. Also from there are the two pieces of ash trays in the front.

The Heart ash tray is part of a set of four depicting each of the card symbols. The Star has an interesting symbol embossed on the back, a large ⊟ enclosing a smaller version of the same (A). One wonders if this might have been an attempt at using another symbol for Akro Agate rather than the flying crow symbol established when the marbles were first made back in 1911.

The heavy green and white ash tray is embossed "Atlantic Foundry," and the eight-pointed star in the back is marked "Victory Safety Tray."

Other pieces included here that are worthy of attention are the hexagonal bowls with ivy motifs at left and right. They are marked "Ramses" and are most likely Westite.

The three chests were called "treasure trunks" by Akro and the pattern number is 804 should you find one marked. They were only made in 1940 and 1941 and were made in a very limited number, so look out for these.

The cold cream jar was found in the Clarksburg area and is typical of the marble-ized Akro swirls; however, there is no proof positive at this writing that it is Akro though I have several similar pieces of jars that were dug up at the factory.

The octagonal plate in the rear has a tumbler ring into which the Westite tumbler fits. The plate, however, is marked Akro.

The large green puff box on the right is pattern 724. The green and white box in the front was found in the Clarksburg area and has definite Akro characteristics, but it is not marked. The cigarette box is a product of pattern 763.

***1992. Things have changed today. The advertising items other than the Hamilton match holder are now more desirable to collectors since they are harder to find!**

* Hamilton match holder	**$40.00**
Hamilton match holder without matches	**$15.00**
3" Ash trays "Edison Hotel"	**$40.00**
3" Ash trays "Lincoln Hotel"	**$40.00**
4" rectangular ash tray "Akro Agate Ware" (embossed inside)	**$100.00**
4½" Hexagonal ash tray "Atlantic Foundry"	**$125.00**
Goodrich ash tray and tire	**$35.00**
Goodrich pen holder & tire	**$60.00**
"Victory" 8 pointed star ash tray	**$200.00**
Bridge set ash trays, 3"	**$400.00**
"Ramses" ivy bowl, 4¼" hexagonal	**$15.00**
"Ramses" bowl covered	**$40.00**
Tray for tumbler and tumbler (marked)	**$100.00**
Treasure trunk (2 styles)	**$75.00**
Cigarette Box 3½" x 4"	**$60.00**
Puff Box, 5" heavy	**$60.00**
Powder Jar with nudes (not Akro but of foreign manufacture)	

* Black – $65.00
No price will be listed for other items until origins of glass are determined.

• CHILDREN'S DISHES (OPAQUES) •

Akro Agate Opaques had the longest run of any of the children's pieces. Beginning in 1935 and continuing until 1947 or 1948, the Opaques spanned a complete range of the color spectrum in varied shapes and sizes.

Jade Akro Luster and Pink Akro Luster were the first attempts at Opaque sets. The names given here are the actual names assigned by Akro Agate for what we now refer to as the "Interior Panel" sets in those colors.

Lusters of pink and jade are pictured. They were made in both small and large sizes, but the smaller size is seemingly more difficult to locate now. In looking for them, many of you will confirm that the pink is in short supply. There are probably fewer of these pink and jade luster sets than of any of the one color opaque sets due to the fact that it's older and had a longer period of usage and, also, there was not much of it made during its two year trial in 1935 and 1936. The green jade luster was more copiously produced than the pink.

The "Little American Maid Set" was introduced in 1937 as an opaque line with mixed colors after initially introducing the Trans-Optics. These mixed color sets seem to have caught on pretty well, which may be another reason for the solid color sets lasting only a couple of years.

By far the most interesting of all the Akro sets is the "Raised Daisy" set as it is the only set with any design or embossing on it. The advanced collectors I have talked with over the last two years feel it to be the most difficult of all to come by. I realize there's a lot of sentiment to the effect that the lemonade and oxblood sets are the rarest of all, but personally, from my own experience, I'm inclined to agree that the "Raised Daisy" is much more difficult than the lemonade and oxblood.

At first, I was not even aware of the existence of a sugar and creamer in the "Raised Daisy" Pattern, but as you can see in the photo, they do exist in at least two colors. Thus far, three colors of lidless teapots have been found, green and two shades of blue, one of which I refer to as sky blue and the other has an aqua hue. Both of these are in the original boxed sets which, by the way, have turned up in 7, 13, and 19 piece sets. The cup has been found only in green and blue. A few blue saucers have also been found.

The dark blue plate in front is the only one of that color I've seen; all the tumblers have been yellow. Saucers and creamers and sugars have shown up in yellow and beige, but you won't see too many sugars and creamers to talk about unless you have a streak of exceptional luck. I have no idea why the teapot in this set has no lid. (Pitcher?)

As more people become aware of this set, more colors may emerge. I would speculate that there might be beige colored tumblers and blue cups. That's part of the excitement of looking — hoping to find something different. My luck has been to find more individual pieces in Nashville, Tennessee. The larger boxed set shown came from North Carolina from a toy store someone had bought out. It cost me a bundle of teal Doric and Pansy; but the set is a real jewel, so don't forget it.

Akro Luster

(Small size)	JADE	PINK	(Large size)	JADE	PINK
Creamer, 1¼"	$25.00	$25.00	Cereal, 3⅜"	$15.00	$20.00
Cup, 1¼"	$10.00	$15.00	Creamer, 1⅜"	$17.50	$22.50
Plate, 3¼"	$7.00	$9.00	Cup, 1⅜"	$12.50	$22.50
Saucer, 2¾"	$5.00	$8.00	Plate, 4¼"	$8.00	$12.00
Sugar, no lid, 1¼"	$25.00	$25.00	Saucer, 3⅛"	$4.00	$7.50
Teapot w/ lid, 2⅜"	$20.00	$22.50	Sugar w/lid, 1⅜"	$25.00	$30.00
Set 16 piece in box	$170.00	$215.00	Teapot w/lid, 2⅝'	$35.00	$45.00
			Set 21 piece in box	$250.00	$365.00

Raised Daisy	OPAQUE SOLID COLORS		OPAQUE SOLID COLORS
Creamer, 1³⁄₁₆"	$80.00	Sugar, 1³⁄₁₆"	$80.00
* Cup, 1³⁄₁₆"	$20.00	Teapot, no lid, 2⅜"	$35.00
Plate, 3"	$15.00	Tumbler, 2"	$25.00
** Saucer, 2½"	$10.00	Set 13 piece in box	$235.00
* Blue $35.00		Set 19 piece in box	$495.00
** Blue $15.00			

• CHILDREN"S DISHES (OPAQUES) •
(Octagonal)

The "Octagonal" design is the most plentiful shape in Akro Agate; it is also one of the most colorful. The top picture shows the supposedly more common "closed" or "solid" handle design. Why, "everyone" says the solid handle octagonal is easily found! It is true that the closed handle in the larger size is more common, but look in the lower right for the lonely three pieces of small size, closed handle octagonal that I have found. Either the small size, closed handle is extremely rare and "everyone" is wrong, or I have searched the wrong areas.

The teapot and sugar bowl with decals were bought for a friend in a lot at a dollar each before I started buying it for myself. I was able to borrow them to photograph for you since I've not seen any more, anywhere, any time. Sound familiar? These sets appear to have decals only on the teapot, creamer and sugar.

Don't do a trick I did when I first started buying Akro Agate: I would only buy sets where the creamer and sugar matched. I found out while working on this book that even boxed sets at the factory did not always have matching pieces. If a set were being packed and matching creamers and sugars were not available, then whatever could be found was stuck in the box. You might even find two different colored cups in a set of four if one color was unavailable at the time of packaging.

The open handled Octagonal, if for no other reason than its vulnerability to break-age, is harder to locate than the closed handle Octagonal (except in the small size as explained above) in the open handled Octagonal design. Since photographing, I have found a chartreuse Octagonal tumbler to bring the total to six different colors found. I've never seen a blue tumbler though there should be some some place.

You might note that except for depth it would be possible to interchange saucers of the larger size Octagonal for the plate in the smaller size because they have the same measurements. However, if you will look closely in each picture, you will see that the saucers for the large size have a degree of depth to them that the plates in the small size do not approximate. Thus, size of items, alone, is not the only criterion to be reckoned with.

The boxed set of pitcher and tumblers actually came with three different colored tumblers. I replaced the white and creme colored tumblers with yellow ones for photographic purposes.

Originally, the "tumbler" was a toothpick holder in the Akro line. Once again they saved the cost of making a new mould by using a mould they already had. All they then had to design was a pitcher to go with it to make a child's water set. In order to compete in the field of low cost glassware, it was probably necessary that Akro be economy minded.

	(open handle) ALL COLORS*	(closed handle) ALL COLORS		(open handle) ALL COLORS*	(closed handle) ALL COLORS
(Small size)			**(Large size)**		
Creamer, 1¼"	$17.50	----------	Cereal, 3⅜"	$11.00	$11.00
Cup, 1¼"	$10.00	$25.00	Creamer, 1½"	$20.00	$10.00 *
Pitchers, 2⅞"	$20.00	----------	Cup, 1½"	$15.00	$6.00
Plate, 3⅜"	$7.00	$7.00	Plate, 4¼"	$7.00	$7.00
Saucer, 2¾"	$6.00	$6.00	Saucer, 3⅜"	$4.00	$4.00
Sugar, no lid, 1¼"	$17.50	----------	Sugar, w/ lid, 1½"	$27.50	$17.00 *
Teapot w/ lid, 2⅜"	$20.00	----------	** Teapot w/ lid, 2⅝"	$35.00	$20.00 *
Tumbler, 2"	$12.00	----------	Set 21 piece in box	$245.00	$175.00
Set 21 piece in box	$235.00	----------	* Add 50% to price for decal items		
			** Red – $200.00		

• CHILDREN'S DISHES (CONCENTRIC RING) •

"Concentric Ring" combines so well with another pattern which goes by the name "Concentric Rib" that only confusion results, so I am using only one name. There is such a minor difference in the spacing of the rings that only an intense study will differentiate the two. My purpose here is to help stimulate your collecting instincts with my observations; maybe at some later date we can split hairs.

While "Concentric Ring" reportedly comes in only the small size, you can see the larger size pictured, including bowls. This was one of my earlier finds in Akro Agate. In fact, my first "Raised Daisy" set and this set were obtained by trading a Blue Cherry child's set in Depression Glass for the two. At the time, it was a foolish trade, but in the end, it has given me more pleasure and started me on more treasure hunts than that child's set in Blue Cherry would ever have done. There is a tremendous range of colors, as you can see. Now is the time to start digging these out of the attic at grandma's to see what you or your mom had back in the 1940's.

You will see the similarities in colors between the larger size sets and the smaller size ones. However, there is a slight change in the shade of blue and the addition of cereals in the larger set. Both sets have the desirable "pumpkin" color cups. I wonder how many boxed sets with lilac colored cups have shown up.

The smaller set on the right is found quite often and many times comes in green and white. This is one of the sets in Akro for which there is very little demand. The green and white color combination seems to go wanting unless the price is very reasonable. Of course, even a small set with four colors would have more appeal than one of just two.

The blue cup on the yellow saucer, as well as the one to its right on the pink saucer, are both unusual shades of Akro. It would pay to be aware of these as well as the lovely lilac shade.

What new color may show up is anybody's guess, so be on the lookout for them. Variety was certainly "the spice" at Akro.

	GREEN WHITE	ALL OTHER OPAQUE COLORS
(Small size)		
Creamer, 1¼"	$7.50	$10.00
*Cup, 1¼"	$4.00	$7.50 *
Plate 3¼"	$2.00 **	$6.00
Saucer, 2¾"	$2.50	$4.50
Sugar, no lid, 1¼"	$7.50	$10.00
Teapot with Lid, 2⅜"	$10.00	$17.50
Set 16 piece in box	$70.00	$125.00

	ALL COLORS
(Large size – rare!)	
Cereal, 3⅜"	$22.50
Creamer, 1⅜"	$25.00
Cup, 1⅜"	$20.00
Plate, 4¼"	$10.00
***Saucer, 3⅛"	$8.00
Sugar with lid, 1⅜"	$35.00
Teapot with lid, 2⅞"	$40.00
Set 21 piece in box	$365.00

* Lavender $30.00; pumpkin $15.00; turquoise $20.00; white $30.00; yellow $40.00.

** Lavender $17.50; turquoise $17.50

*** Red $50.00

• CHILDREN'S DISHES (STACKED DISC) •

The common name "Stacked Disc" will have to suffice for now; it does describe the graduated bands up the side of each piece that isn't flat, though "inverted steps" or "beehive" or something would be easier to remember. There is a band of six wide circles on each saucer and plate. You will find that some saucers have an indent for the cup and some do not. Ours is not to wonder why as there are already enough unanswered questions.

Notice that this pattern is the same on the outside as that of "Stacked Disc and Panel." However, each piece is smooth on the inside rather than panelled. Too, this was not one of Akro's more vivid patterns. There's a possibility of a colorful set with the orange, yellow and pink, but for the most part, the pieces are not as colorful as some of the other patterns. You might notice the translucency of the white teapot in the center. Pieces like this show the variety that even a single color can provide in Akro. Akro used a tiny flower pot mould for making the tumbler in this pattern and thus had only to design a pitcher to make the water set for the "Stacked Disc."

	SOLID GREEN SOLID WHITE	OTHER OPAQUE COLORS	PINK
Creamer, 1¼"	$7.00	$10.00	$20.00
Cup, 1¼"	$4.00	$6.00 *	$40.00
Pitcher, 2⅞"	$10.00	$14.00	----------
Plate, 3¼"	$2.00	$5.00	$20.00
Saucer, 2¾"	$2.00	$4.00	----------
Sugar, no lid, 1¼"	$7.00	10.00	$20.00
Teapot with lid, 2⅜"	$12.00	$14.00	$14.00
Tumbler, 2"	$4.50	$8.00	$8.00
Set 16 piece in box	$80.00	$105.00	----------
Set 8 piece in box	$32.50	$55.00	----------

*Yellow $45.00

• CHILDREN'S DISHES (INTERIOR PANEL) •

Using the same pattern made for the Akro Jade and Pink Lusters, now commonly referred to as "Interior Panel," Akro later expanded the color scheme, for which collectors are grateful. You have to admit that a mixed set of these later colors, or even a solid set of blue, would beat the old green or pink. All of these pieces fit the "Interior Panel" common name description. Pieces are "paneled" on the interior, or on the top of flat pieces. Notice that again some of the teapots, creamers and sugars as in the marbleized sets have the darts while others have smooth exteriors.

The range of color that takes place in Akro Agate is seen nowhere as vividly as in the varying shades of yellow and orange. I'd like a complete set of the orange and white shown in the center. However, so far, I've only found one saucer. Collectors have taken to calling the orangelike color "pumpkin." Maybe, like Linus, I can hope the "Great Pumpkin" will rise out of the pumpkin patch and bring me the goodies I'm hoping for.

Pumpkin and the deep cobalt blue shown would seem to be those most desired by collectors, so keep this in mind when premium prices are asked. Color does make a difference in most cases.

(Stacked Disc and Panel)

I have placed the "Stacked Disc and Panel" here so that the differences between it and "Interior Panel" may be easily seen. Not only does the "Stacked Disc and Panel" have interior panels, but the exterior has a stacked band of ridges. Notable here is the tumbler which is not often seen in opaque but is quite common in the Trans-Optic green.* Looking from the top, there is no difference in the plates and saucers, but if you turn the "Stacked Disc and Panel" over, there will be a ridge or two around the back. You might see this ridge on the yellow cereal if you look closely enough.

Again, the teapot slopes inward at the base, whereas the pitcher is straight all the way to the base. This will help the novice to separate a topless tea pot from a pitcher.

Both "Interior Panel" and "Stacked Disc and Panel" come boxed in an endless variety of color schemes. To me, getting a set of varied colors adds something more to the set than getting one of just solid color. This, of course, is a matter of individual taste. The real problem is just to find it in the first place.

*Pitcher shown is "Stacked Disc."

TOP RIGHT PAGE 55:

Interior Panel

(Small Size)	COBALT/ PUMPKIN	SOLID COLORS	(Large Size)	COBALT/ PUMPKIN	SOLID COLORS
Creamer, 1¼"	$25.00	$20.00	Cereal, 3⅜"	----------	$22.50
Cup, 1¼"	$20.00	$18.00	Creamer, 1⅜"	$25.00	$25.00
Plate, 3¼"	----------	$7.50	Cup, 1⅜"	$20.00	$15.00
Saucer, 2¾"	----------	$10.00	Plate 4¼"	----------	$10.00
Sugar, No Lid, 1¼"	$25.00	$20.00	Saucer, 3⅛"	----------	$7.00
Teapot with lid, 2⅜"	$35.00	$25.00	Sugar with lid, 1⅜"	$40.00	$37.50
16 piece set in box	----------	$225.00	Teapot with lid, 2⅝"	$40.00	$40.00
			21 piece set in box	----------	$335.00

SEE OPPOSITE PAGE FOR PRICES

Stacked Disc and Panel

(Small Size)	COBALT/ PUMPKIN	SOLID COLORS	(Large Size – Very Rare!)	ALL SOLID COLORS
Creamer, 1¼"	$25.00	$12.00	Cereal, 3⅜"	$35.00
Cup, 1¼"	$20.00	$10.00	Creamer 1⅜"	$25.00
Plate, 3¼"	-----------	$10.00	Cup, 1⅜"	$20.00
Saucer, 2¾"	-----------	$8.00	Plate, 4¼"	$10.00
Sugar, no lid, 1¼"	$25.00	$12.00	Saucer, 3⅛"	$8.00
Teapot with lid, 2⅝"	$35.00	$25.00	Sugar with lid, 1⅝"	$32.50
Set 16 piece in box	-----------	$180.00	Teapot with lid, 2⅝"	$40.00
			Tumbler, 2"	$50.00
			Set 21 piece in box	$410.00

• CHILDREN'S DISHES (J. PRESSMAN AKRO) •

I have tried everything to convince myself that Akro did not make these crudely shaped child's dishes known more commonly as "Chiquita," but I have been unable to do so. Plant workers remember them, and there are a lot of pieces that have been found in the Clarksburg, West Virginia, area.

The common color of Chiquita is the green shown in the large 21 piece set, but the blue is frequently found also. People seem to prefer the blue color; therefore, the price, because of demand, has grown to be greater than for green. Other colors of Chiquita — lilac, turquoise, pastel blue — are much more rare but not as avidly sought. Some collectors of Akro have never seen anything except the blue and green Chiquita.

All Chiquita, if it bears a mark, has a *J.P.* embossed on the bottom, because it was made for the J. Pressman Company of New York. They must have given Akro a tremendous amount of business because if the Chiquita is not the most often found Akro, then it runs a close second.

Both the turquoise and pastel blue teapots are lidless in the picture. I am also missing creamers in two of the colors, actually all three since the pastel blue creamer is borrowed. I have never seen a lilac teapot, but it may exist. If anyone has a boxed set with the lilac cups and yellow saucers, I would like to know what color teapot, creamer and sugar were packed with it.

Apparently rare, but not exactly as pretty as it is colorful, is the set of baked-on Chiquita shown in the lower photograph. The four colors are baked-on over a crystal base which leads one to believe that crystal pieces could exist. All the surrounding items bear the J.P. mark and exhibit a range of colors not shown

in any other Akro pieces. The molasses or brownish transparent color on the left seems to be quite scarce; several collectors of many years standing did not even know it existed. You will find that even these fat shaped J.P. pieces didn't escape the barrage of baked on colors that captured the Chiquita. I have seen a 5 piece set of these minus the creamer in which the cups were red, saucers were yellow, plates were green and the teapot, sugar and most likely the creamer were blue just as in the baked on Chiquita pieces. The cereal bowl in red remains a mystery as there were five in this set, thus suggesting that they may exist in red in the Chiquita sets also.

The only example of transparent blue I could find was the creamer, but I have seen a couple of completed sets in private collections. The dark green is a shade not found in any other Akro pieces to date. Surprising to me is the fact that I have found three green creamers with lids. The creamer and sugar have the same inside diameter and thus the lids could have been interchangeable. Whether lids were actually made for the creamer will have to be a guess until a boxed set turns up. It seems significant to have found three in three different locations all with lids, though.

Although the shapes and colors of all the J.P. items leave a lot to be desired in many collector's thinking, you may find that these are the sleepers of the Akro Agate line. They are not plentiful, and previous publications on Akro have only included the Chiquita items. Want a challenge? Try to find a completed set of the larger pieces within six months of reading about them.

Chiquita	OPAQUE GREEN	TRANSPARENT COBALT*	BAKED-ON COLORS		OPAQUE GREEN	TRANSPARENT COBALT*	BAKED-ON COLORS
Cereal, 3¾"	----------	----------	----------	Saucer, 3⅛"	2.00	$4.00	$5.00
Creamer, 1½"	$5.00	$12.00	$8.00	Sugar, no lid, 1½"	$5.00	$12.00	$8.00
Cup, 1½"	$4.00	$12.00	$7.00	Teapot with lid, 2¾"	$10.00	$20.00	$15.00
Plate, 3¾"	$3.00	$15.00	$6.00	Set 16 pieces in box	$67.50	$100.00 (12 pcs)	
				Set 22 piece in set	$100.00	$160.00	$135.00 (20 pcs)

*Double prices for the other opaque colors

J.P. (Large Size)	TRANSPARENT BROWN OR GREEN	TRANSPARENT BLUE	BAKED-ON COLORS	(Large Size)	TRANSPARENT BROWN OR GREEN	TRANSPARENT BLUE	BAKED-ON COLORS
Cereal, 3¹³⁄₁₆"	----------	----------	$8.00	Saucer, 3¼"	$10.00	$12.00	$5.00
Creamer, 1½"	$25.00	$35.00	$10.00	Sugar with lid, 12½"	$40.00	45.00	$15.00
Cup, 1½"	$20.00	$30.00	$8.00	Teapot with lid, 2¾"	$50.00	$65.00	$25.00
Plate, 4¼"	$12.00	$15.00	$6.00	Set 16 piece in box	$300.00	$400.00	$180.00(20 pcs)

• CHILDREN'S DISHES ONYX (MARBLEIZED) •

Akro used *onyx* to describe what we now call marbleized. *Marbleized* means that the color goes completely through the glass, but the colorful swirls of Akro Agate are surface or near surface swirls. The only truly Marbleized Akro Agate is the orange and white on the following page. No matter what the two tone color of Akro Agate actually is in composition, the fact remains that it is the most avidly sought type by collectors and as such, it is likely to be elusive.

To me, the variations in pattern are not as important a factor as the color in the Marbleized Akro. For instance, the picture at the right shows a blend of three different patterns, but you have to look for the distinctions as it's the blue and white color combination that is striking here, rather than the design. I guess what I'm saying here is that in the Marbleized, you can get away with an interchange of patterns and it's all right if the color is right. This way, you can complete your "set" with less agony and still have a pleasing display.

For the sticklers, the bowls in the back which appear to be the same pattern, but aren't, are "Interior Panel" on the right and "Stacked Disc and Panel" on the left. This becomes important only since a marbleized "Stacked Disc and Panel" bowl has never been previously listed. Both large and small sizes of "Concentric Ring" are shown in the foreground. I have only found this pattern in the blue-white or blue-creme combinations, but tomorrow you may find it in oxblood-white or green-white. Who knows!

Looking at the lower photo, you can see the other two colors found with white. You may notice a distinct lack of large size green and white pieces as I couldn't find any, but I did picture both styles of teapots, creamers, and sugars with the small size "Interior Panel" set. Take a look at the darts or rays so common to these pieces. Now, the perfectly plain pieces in front came from another set packed in the same style box as the one shown. To have darts or not to have darts just seems to be another of those unexplained occurrences in Akro pieces.

The oxblood-white combination is shown in both sizes, but all the pieces are "Interior Panel." Except for large size green and white, I had more trouble locating pieces of marbleized in oxblood-white. In "Interior Panel," the small size sugars do not have lids, while the large size does. Keep your eyes open since you might be the first to discover one of these two marbleized colors in some pattern other than "Interior Panel."

Marbleized (Small Size)	Prices are listed by size and color and not pattern		
	BLUE-WHITE	OXBLOOD-WHITE	GREEN-WHITE
Creamer, 1¼"	$35.00	$32.50	$25.00
Cup, 1¼"	$30.00	$25.00	$20.00
Plate, 3¼"	$15.00	$13.00	$12.50
Saucer, 2⅜"	$12.00	$9.00	$8.00
Sugar, 1¼"	$35.00	$32.50	$25.00
Teapot with lid, 2⅜"	$40.00	$37.50	$35.00
Set 16 piece in box	$360.00	$310.00	$265.00
(Large Size)			
Cereal, 3⅜"	$32.50	$27.50	$22.50
Ceamer, 1⅜"	$32.50	$27.50	$22.50
Cup, 1⅜"	$32.50	$25.00	$20.00
Plate, 4¼"	$18.00	$12.50	$12.00
Saucer, 3¼"	$15.00	$10.00	$8.00
Sugar with lid, 1⅜"	$45.00	$40.00	$40.00
Teapot with lid, 2⅝"	$65.00	$55.00	$45.00
Set 21 piece in box	$515.00	$435.00	$380.00

Akro Agate

• CHILDREN'S DISHES (MISS AMERICA) •

The true marbleized set of orange-white shown here might well be Akro's rarest child's set. All of the pieces on this page are the creme de la creme of Akro if you choose collector's demand as a guide. Very few even know the orange-white or the forest green Akro Agate exist. I understand that plates have been found in the forest green; I have four cups and saucers, so we're on the way to a set! For the dis-believers, I'll hasten to add that both colors are marked with a crow on some pieces though others just have pattern numbers.

The solid white is collectible, but it is more desirable with the decal on the pieces.

Why so few decal pieces remain is a mystery unless it was so time consuming a process at the factory that few were made. These sets have been dubbed "Miss America" by collectors, so we shall stick to that for now.

I stumbled over both the dark green and the orange-white when I first started buying Akro Agate for the Depression Glass book and, although I have looked for almost two years now, I have not seen another piece of either. These sets look more like children's dishes than nearly any of the other sets possible due to the open handles, larger size and the basically heavier quality.

(Large Size)	WHITE	DECAL	ORANGE-WHITE	GREEN
Creamer	$35.00	$52.50	$75.00	----------
Cup	$32.50	$45.00	$60.00	$60.00
Plate	$20.00	$30.00	$37.50	$30.00
Saucer	$15.00	$25.00	$30.00	$25.00
Sugar with lid	$65.00	$80.00	$110.00	----------
Teapot with lid	$100.00	$135.00	$150.00	----------
Set in box (17 piece)	$475.00	$675.00	$875.00	$460.00 *

*12 piece set

• CHILDREN'S DISHES (LEMONADE AND OXBLOOD) •

The "Lemonade and Oxblood," as the yellow-red combination has been dubbed, comes in two basic shapes: the round, large size "Interior Panel" and the large size "Octagonal" with closed handles. More collectors are searching for these sets than any other Akro Agate set, marbleized or otherwise because "everyone" knows that this is the hardest thing in Akro to find. Well, I'm swimming up-stream, I know, but I think the "Raised Daisy" rates this distinction. Be that as it may, many collectors have seen few if any pieces in this color.

Collectors have varying opinions as to which of the two sets, "Interior Panel" or "Octagon," is the most difficult to find. Personally, I've had more difficulty in finding the octagonal pieces, but I have seen several completed sets of both. I would inject here that the time to buy hard-to-find items is when you see them, provided the price fits your pocketbook, of course.

My personal observation is that this set, in comparison to other Akro sets, is too highly priced for its scarcity. Demand has caused it to be one of Akro's highest priced sets. It usually takes both ingredients — scarcity and demand — for prices to spiral in glassware.

If you look closely at the plates in the back, you can see the swirled effect of the red on both sides of the plate. If it were marbleized in the true sense of the word, it would appear as one swirl and not as two separate ones.

Lemonade and oxblood appears in another item in this book, as an ash tray. Amazingly, that piece has a satin-like finish to it.

Lemonade and Oxblood

	INTERIOR PANEL	OCTAGONAL
Cereal, 3⅜"	$30.00	$25.00
Creamer, 1⅜"	$35.00	----------
Creamer, 1½"	----------	$30.00
Cup, 1⅜"	$25.00	----------
Cup, 1½"	----------	$25.00
Plate, 4¼"	$20.00	$20.00
Saucer, 3⅛"	$12.50	----------
Saucer, 3⅜"	----------	$12.50
Sugar with lid, 1⅜"	$55.00	----------
Sugar, no lid, 1½"	----------	$35.00
Teapot with lid, 2⅝"	$67.50	$67.50
Set in box (21 piece)	$525.00	$485.00

• CHILDREN'S DISHES
(TOPAZ, TRANS-OPTIC, 1935 – 36) •

The name given by Akro Agate to the children's line of transparent glassware was Trans-Optic. There was no distinction made by the company as to pattern names of the transparent sets; therefore, the common names given before ("Concentric Ring," "Stippled Band" etc.) should suffice for now.

The layout of these pictures for children's pieces was my idea so that you could see different pieces and different patterns all at once. To me, it becomes more readily identifiable if you can compare all at one time in one picture. I hope you agree.

The topaz Trans-Optic turns out to be the rarest of all Akro Agate Trans-Optics. It was made ony in 1935 and 1936, so there are few sets available since it was not generally accepted by the public. You will note that there are two basic patterns shown, which have been commonly called "Stippled Band"
and "Interior Panel." Noteworthy is the fact that it is extremely difficult to match up pieces in color. There are two distinct shades of topaz in each pattern. Another pattern which combines the stippling on the outside and the panels on the inside has been called "Stippled Interior Panel." Actually, the panels seem to dominate, so I am considering this pattern as part of the "Interior Panel" pattern.

You will have great difficulty in finding sugars and creamers in this set, as evidenced by the lack of any creamers here. Remember that the larger sets have sugar lids but the smaller sets do not. The topaz, as other sets, came in 8,10,14,16, 21, and even a few 28 piece sets. In fact, in 1935 Akro made 477 of the 28 piece sets. If you own one, consider yourself lucky as it's doubtful many sets survived intact. You may find a 7 piece water set hard to locate also.

(Small Size)	INTERIOR PANEL	STIPPLED INTERIOR PANEL	STIPPLED BAND
Creamer, 1¼"	$25.00	$30.00	$25.00
Cup, 1¼"	$15.00	$20.00	$7.00
Plate, 3¼"	$9.00	$15.00	$4.00
Saucer, 2¾"	$7.50	$12.50	$3.00
Sugar, no lid, 1¼"	$25.00	$30.00	$25.00
Teapot and lid, 2⅜"	$30.00	$35.00	$18.00
Set in box (16 piece)	$225.00	$300.00	$125.00
(Large Size)			
Cereal, 3⅜"	$17.50	----------	
Creamer, 1⅜"	$15.00	----------	
Creamer, 1½"	----------	$15.00	
Cup, 1⅜"	$13.50	----------	
Cup, 1½"	----------	$11.00	
Pitcher, 2⅞"	$20.00	$18.00	
Plate, 4½"	$8.50	$7.00	
Saucer, 3⅛"	$5.00	----------	
Saucer, 3¼"	---------	$5.00	
Sugar, with lid, 1⅜"	$30.00	----------	
Sugar with lid, 1½"	----------	$25.00	
Teapot, with lid, 2⅝"	$35.00	$30.00	
Tumbler 2"	$15.00	$20.00	
Tumbler, 1¹¹⁄₁₆"	----------	$10.00	
21 Piece set in box	$280.00	----------	
17 Piece set in box	$210.00	$180.00	

• CHILDREN'S DISHES (JADE TRANS-OPTIC) •

This is where the test of putting all the same color together to emphasize the differences in patterns will meet its first obstacle. The Jade Trans-Optic was made from 1935 through 1938. There are four different patterns in this picture. At left front is the "Stippled Band" while "Interior Panel" is in the two boxed sets from the left. "Stacked Disc and Panel" makes up the boxed water set on the right as well as the center of the picture, and the "Stippled Interior Panel" is shown on the right. I hope you can see the differences from the common names. There should not be much difficulty except in the "Stippled Interior Panel" and the "Interior Panel"; this will be a problem only in the small sizes since the "Stippled Interior Panel" was only made in the small size. The stippled effect is on the outside and the panels are on the inside with the stippling just like that of the "Stippled Band" set. Personally, I think you can combine this into "Interior Panel" without anyone noticing or possibly caring.

The Jade Trans-Optic is the easiest to get of the Trans-Optics, but the small sizes are a little more difficult to assemble. There is a possibility of running into two shades of green in completing your sets, as the "Stacked Disc and Panel" has a more yellow cast in some of the small size pieces shown. This will not always hold true, so you will have to keep it in mind when ordering by mail or when out shopping without a sample piece along.

The seven piece water sets in green are the most commonly found, but boxed sets are bringing premium prices regardless of the availability. Boxed water sets are bringing $5.00 to $7.50 more than the separate items provided the boxes are in good condition. Many collectors feel that the boxes take up too much display room. But if you have the room available, it seems the only way to go is to show the original packaging — which may even include its original much lesser price!

	INTERIOR PANEL STACKED DISC & PANEL	STIPPLED INTERIOR PANEL
(Small Size)		
Creamer, 1¼"	**$30.00**	**$32.50**
Cup, 1¼"	**$15.00**	**$17.50**
Pitcher, 2⅞"	**$17.50**	**$25.00**
Plate, 3¼"	**$8.00**	**$12.00**
Saucer, 3¾"`	**$6.00**	**$10.00**
Sugar, no lid, 1¼"	**$30.00**	**$32.50**
Teapot with lid, 2⅜"	**$25.00**	**$30.00**
Tumbler, 1¹¹⁄₁₆"	----------	**$12.50**
Tumbler, 2"	**$10.00**	
Set 16 piece in box	**$215.00**	**$275.00**
(Large Size)		**STIPPLED BAND**
Cereal, 3⅜"	**$20.00**	----------
Creamer, 1⅜"	**$15.00**	----------
Creamer, 1½"	----------	**$15.00**
Cup, 1⅜"	**$11.00**	----------
Cup, 1½"	----------	**$9.00**
Plate, 4¼"	**$8.00**	**$8.00**
Saucer, 3⅛"	**(I.P.)$4.00**	----------
Saucer, 3¼"	**(S.D.)$12.00**	**$4.00**
Sugar with lid, 1⅜"	**$30.00**	----------
Sugar with lid, 1½"	----------	**$25.00**
Teapot with lid, 2⅝"	**$35.00**	**$30.00**
Set 21 piece in box	**$280.00**	----------
Set 17 piece in box	**$200.00**	**$170.00**

• CHILDREN'S DISHES (AZURE TRANS-OPTIC) •

The boxed set shown (black box with silver lettering "The Little American Maid Tea Set manufactured by the Akro Agate Company of Clarksburg, West Virginia") is one of Akro's first boxed sets. I apologize for the miserable box, but it's the only one like this I have. On the left are the small size pieces of "Stacked Disc and Panel" while on the right are the large size. I have never figured out if pitcher and tumblers go with the large or the small size sets, but I would guess the small size set. Note the straight sides of the pitcher in the left rear as opposed to the tapering of the sides of the teapot in front of it. This little distinction will save headaches when you find a topless teapot and you need a pitcher and already have a teapot with a lid.

The center cup caused me headaches because it comes with the same serving pieces as the "Stacked Disc and Panel" did, but as you can see, it is quite different. The common name, "Concentric Ring," is given here for what it's worth, but surely we can do better than that some day. Only the cups differ in the two patterns. Look at the opaque patterns for another view of "Concentric Ring" and "Stacked Disc and Panel."

Again, you will have trouble finding sugars and creamers as well as the complete boxed sets. Whereas you usually find the amber pieces scattered a piece or two at a time, I have been able to get azure pieces in quantity when I've been lucky enough to find them at all. It seems that the blue has stayed together better for some reason — possibly because people have a fondness for the color blue.

You will note that prices on the blue have reached a higher level than the green or topaz. With more demand for topaz, it's scarcity will surely catch the price up to the price of blue. Remember, no matter how rare a piece is, there has to be a demand to make the price rise.

(Small Size)	STACKED DISC & PANEL	CONCENTRIC RING
Creamer, 1¼"	$35.00	$35.00
Cup, 1¼	$30.00	$30.00
Plate, 3¼"	$15.00	$17.50
Saucer, 2¾"	$12.00	$12.00
Sugar, no lid, 1¼"	$35.00	$35.00
Teapot with lid, 2⅜"	$35.00	$35.00
Set 16 pieces in box	$350.00	$360.00

(Large Size)		STIPPLED BAND
Cereal, 3⅜"	$32.50	----------
Creamer, 1⅜"	$35.00	----------
Creamer, 1½"	----------	$35.00
Cup, 1⅜"	$27.50	----------
Cup, 1½"	----------	$30.00
Pitcher, 2⅞"	$35.00	----------
Plate, 4¼"	$15.00	$17.50
Saucer, 3¼"	$12.00	$15.00
Sugar with lid, 1⅜"	$45.00	----------
Sugar with lid, 1½"	----------	$50.00
Teapot with lid, 2⅝"	$65.00	$65.00
Tumbler, 2"	$15.00	----------
Set 21 piece in box	$515.00	----------
Set 17 piece in box	$385.00	$425.00

Wonderful WESTITE WARE

AN AMERICAN PRODUCT

JARDINIERES

GARDEN DISHES

VASES · BOWLS

J. H. BALMER CO.

399 Central Avenue,
Newark, N. J.

By courtesy of *Florists Exchange and Horticultural Trade World*, a florist trade paper, we quote from an article "Flower Pots for the Public" by Prof. Linus H. Jones in the June 18, 1932 issue.

"The roots in a clay pot are, for the most part, found as a web between the wall of the pot and the soil mass. In a non-porous container, the root system is quite generally distributed throughout the soil. Should the wall of a clay pot dry out, there is grave danger that the roots in its vicinity would also become dry even though the surface of the soil were moist. In a non-porous pot, however, since the soil moisture is quite evenly distributed in the soil, it takes a long time for the soil to become dry."

Note: On page 29 of this issue is an illustration comparing Adiantum in a non-porous pot and a clay one. The non-porous pot is WESTITE and the photograph shows how much better its plant withstood the dry unfavorable atmosphere in an office than the one in the clay pot.

We quote by courtesy of *Better Homes and Gardens* from an article "Some Old Notions Topple" by the same author which appeared in the February, 1933, issue.

"Perhaps the greatest error is the belief that the wall of the clay pot allows air to pass through to aerate the soil. This belief may be responsible for the mistaken opinion that house plants will not thrive in non-porous containers . . .

In pots that do not have evaporating surface, as does the clay pot, soil moisture is evenly distributed throughout the soil mass. There is no porous wall to absorb the moisture needed by the plant. The nutrients are diffused in the soil and are not lost by accumulating in the wall of the pot."

Note: On page 27 of this issue, Photograph 3 compares a fern grown in a non-porous pot with one in a clay pot. The non-porous pot is WESTITE and its plant was not affected by week-end neglect whereas the one in the clay pot withered and died.

2-4-33

WESTITE CATALOG REPRINT

WESTITE is distinctly AMERICAN. It is made from raw materials (taken from the hills of our native land) which are fused by scientific processes with mineral oxides, resulting in a variety of colors and color combinations, no two of which are ever quite alike.

Features of WESTITE ware are:

Colors: Lustrous—Blending—Permanent
Can never fade or deteriorate
Free from dyes

Strength: Durable—Sturdy

Designs: Artistic—Attractive
Graceful—Dignified

Uses: Ideal as settings for growing plants, bulbs and flowers
Excellent as Jardinieres and Vases

Cleansing: Gloss immediately restored by wiping with a damp cloth

Prices: Reasonable

DECORATED WESTITE

In an effort to further improve the appearance of WESTITE, exhaustive research work has been conducted and it is a pleasure to now offer DECORATED WESTITE companionate with WESTITE.

DECORATED WESTITE is produced by affixing to an original piece a befitting design colored to best suit the individuality of the item. It is then fired at a high temperature assuring permanency. DECORATED WESTITE offers many pleasing effects and like WESTITE, no two items are ever exactly alike.

Illustrations of DECORATED WESTITE may be seen on pages 5 and 13 of this booklet.

Prof. Linus H. Jones, of the Massachusetts State College, Amherst, Mass., a recognized authority on plant growth, has conducted exhaustive experiments in the observation of comparative growth of plants and flowers in non-porous containers and ordinary clay pots. The results of his investigations determined that plants and flowers under identical conditions thrive with less care and bloom more freely in non-porous containers than in ordinary pots. They disproved the long standing and accepted belief that plant life could only be sustained in the so-called porous pots and demonstrated that greater success is obtained with the non-porous ones, such as WESTITE.

After a series of 85 tests, each comprising an exacting check on the growth of a like plant or flower in a WESTITE pot and an ordinary one, and in which an effort was made to place the better of the two plants in the ordinary pot, thereby dispelling any claim that more successful results obtained in WESTITE pots could be attributed to a better start at the beginning of each test, Prof. Jones concluded:

"Plants grown on the sills of office windows usually did remarkably well in the Westite pots and poorly in the clay pots. The lack of care during Sundays and holidays particularly if Monday was a holiday contributed greatly to the difference in growth. However, even with average care the plants in the Westite pots did much better than plants in clay pots.

"In homes where care was haphazard, the Westite pots produced superior plants, and in homes where plant management was poorly understood, the plants said that in clay pots and thrived in Westite pots.

"Reports from the various experiments were very complimentary to the Westite pots. Their appearance was much more satisfactory than the appearance of the clay pots. People were very much impressed with the small amount of water necessary to maintain a moist soil, which meant lack of worry when people were away for weekends."

WESTITE pots do not permit the rapid evaporation of the water supplied or the absorption of a large percentage of nitrous plant food necessary and vital to plant life. Ordinary pots do. In addition, Westite pots provide better balance of plant growth owing to better balance of soil moisture and allow flowering plants to bloom more freely and retain their blossoms for a longer period of time.

IMPORTANT: In watering plants in WESTITE pots keep the soil MOIST but never WET.

JARDINIERE
(Stand sold separately)

No.		Inside Top Diameter	Inside Depth	Size	Shipping Weight Per Doz.
299	Jardiniere	1½"	2"		2½ lbs.
300	Jardiniere	2½"	2½"		6 lbs.
301*	Jardiniere	3½"	3½"		11 lbs.
302	Jardiniere	4½"	5"		25 lbs.
303	Jardiniere	6"	6"		56 lbs.
740	Stand used with 299, 300, 301			4" x 4"	12 lbs.
750	Stand used with 302, 303			6" x 6"	20 lbs.

Above items supplied as follows:

299, 303, 750	300, 301, 302, 740
Onyx	Onyx
White	White
Solid Green	Solid Green
Mottled Green	Mottled Green
	Blue

*301 has a cleverly designed feature on the bottom which can be easily and quickly removed where a drain is desired or considered necessary.

4

DECORATED JARDINIERE
(Stand sold separately)

This picture shows the same jardiniere as on the preceding page only in Decorated Westite. It clearly illustrates the improved appearance and added attractiveness given Westite by our decorating process.

While our jardinieres are highly recommended by eminent authorities as pots most desirable for growing plants, etc., they are often used as containers for potted plants. When so used the following numbers are best suitable for the size of the pot given.

No.	Pot
300	2"
301	3"
302	4½" or 4"
303	5"

LIST PRICE EACH

No.	Decorated	Undecorated
299	$ .17	$ .13
300	.18	.14
301	.22	.17
302	.46	.41
303	.85	.72

5

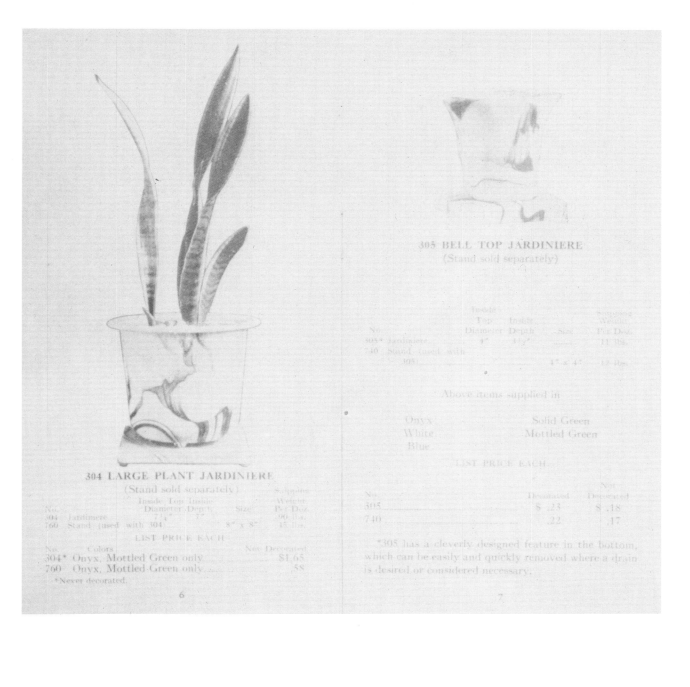

304 LARGE PLANT JARDINIERE
(Stand sold separately)

305 BELL TOP JARDINIERE
(Stand sold separately)

VASE
(Stand sold separately)

No.	Inside Top Diameter	Inside Depth	Size	Shipping Weight Per Doz.
310 Vase	2⅜"	6½"		15 lbs.
311 Vase	3¼"	7¼"		24 lbs.
750 Stand (used with 310 or 311)			6" x 6"	20 lbs.

Above items supplied in

Onyx	Solid Green
White	Mottled Green

LIST PRICE EACH

No.	Decorated	Not Decorated
310	$ .42	$ .34
311	.70	.55
750	.41	.36

8

312 VASE
(Stand sold separately)

No.	Inside Top Diameter	Inside Depth	Size	Shipping Weight Per Doz.
312 Vase	4½"	7¾"		35 lbs.
750 Stand (used with 312)			6" x 6"	20 lbs.

Above items supplied in

Onyx	Solid Green
White	Mottled Green

LIST PRICE EACH

No.	Decorated	Not Decorated
312	$ .95	$ .75
750	.41	.36

9

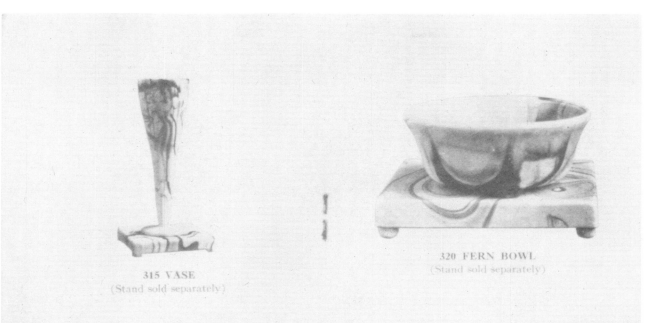

315 VASE
(Stand sold separately)

320 FERN BOWL
(Stand sold separately)

No.	Inside Top Diameter	Inside Depth	Size	Shipping Weight Per Doz.
315 Vase	2⅜"	5½"		1¾ lbs.
740 Stand (used with 315)			4" x 4"	1? lbs.

No.	Inside Top Diameter	Inside Depth	Size	Shipping Weight Per Doz.
320 Fern Bowl	4⅝"	1⅝"		12 lbs.
750 Stand (used with 320)			6" x 6"	20 lbs.

Above items supplied in

Onyx   Solid Green

White   Mottled Green

LIST PRICE EACH

No.	Decorated	Not Decorated
315	$ .42	$ .34
740	.22	.17

10

Above items supplied in

Onyx   Solid Green

White   Mottled Green

LIST PRICE EACH

No.	Decorated	Not Decorated
320	$ .22	$ .17
750	.41	.36

11

BULB BOWL
(Stand sold separately)

No.	Inside Top Diameter	Inside Depth	Size	Shipping Weight Per Doz.
330	Bulb Bowl			20 lbs.
331	Bulb Bowl			35 lbs.
750	Stand (used with 330)		6" x 6"	30 lbs.
760	Stand (used with 331)		8" x 8"	45 lbs.

Above items supplied in

Onyx	Solid Green
White	Mottled Green

LIST PRICE EACH

No.	Not Decorated
330	$ 48
331	58
750	36
760	58

12

DECORATED BULB BOWL
(Stand sold separately)

This is an illustration of the same bowl as on preceding page only in Decorated Westite. It also shows a decorated stand.

These decorations add considerably to the appearance and attractiveness of these and all Westite pieces.

LIST PRICE EACH

No.	Decorated
330	$ 45
331	70
750	44
760	65

13

340 NASTURTIUM BOWL
(Stand sold separately)

No.		Inside Top Diameter	Inside Depth	Size	Shipping Weight Per Doz.
340	Bowl	5½"	2½"		15 lbs.
750	Stand (used with 340)			6" x 6"	20 lbs.

Above items supplied in

Onyx	Solid Green
White	Mottled Green

LIST PRICE EACH

No.		Decorated	Not Decorated
340		$ .22	$ .17
750		.41	.36

14

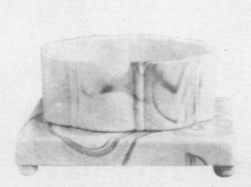

350 PANSY BOWL
(Stand sold separately)

No.		Inside Top Diameter	Inside Depth	Size	Shipping Weight Per Doz.
350	Bowl	4½"	2½"		15 lbs.
750	Stand (used with 350)			6" x 6"	20 lbs.

Above items supplied in

Onyx	Solid Green
White	Mottled Green

LIST PRICE EACH

No.		Decorated	Not Decorated
350		$ .40	$ .34
750		.41	.36

15

360 IVY BOWL
(Stand sold separately)

600 GARDEN DISH
(Stand sold separately)

No.		Inside Top Diameter	Inside Depth	Size	Shipping Weight Per Doz.
360	Bowl	3¼"	1½"		15 lbs.
750	Stand (used with				
750				6" x 6"	24 lbs.

Above items supplied in

Onyx   Solid Green
White   Mottled Green

LIST PRICE EACH

No.	Decorated	Not Decorated
360	$ .40	$ .34
750	.41	.36

No.		Inside Top Diameter	Inside Depth	Size	Shipping Weight Per Doz.
600	Dish	7½"	1½"		45 lbs.
760	Stand (used with				
600				8" x 8"	45 lbs.

Above items supplied in

Onyx   Solid Green
White   Mottled Green

LIST PRICE EACH

No.	Not Decorated
600*	$ .88
760	.58

*Never Decorated.

16   17

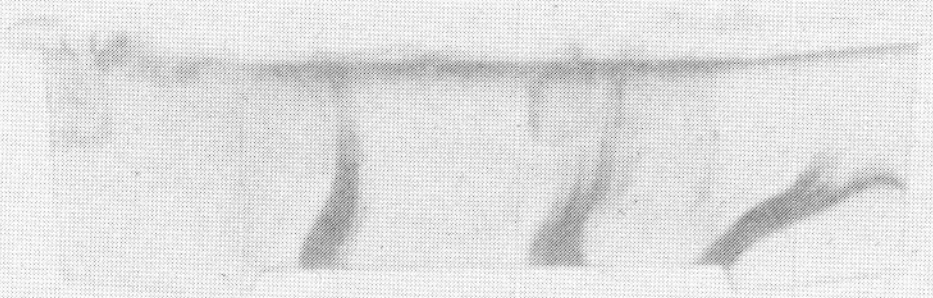

650 GARDEN DISH
(Japanese Type)

Inside Length	Inside Width at Center	Inside Depth	Shipping Weight Per Doz.
10"	5½"	1½"	48 lbs.

Supplied only in

Onyx

Mottled Green

Never Decorated

List Price Each

$1.20

18

(Aquariums not for sale)

We neither manufacture nor sell aquariums. This illustration is intended to show the possibilities of ornamentation with WESTITE AGATES.

WESTITE is crushed into various sizes to produce WESTITE AGATES after which the agates are tumbled to remove sharp edges. Their colors are permanent and will not injure the most delicate fish.

WESTITE AGATES are supplied in small mesh bags each weighing approximately 22 ounces. (One gross mesh bags weigh approximately 200 lbs.)

No.	Description	Use	List Price Per Bag
2	Medium	For decorating potted plants. Mixed with No. 3 in aquariums	$ .08
3	Coarse	For Bulbs	.08
4	Very Coarse	For large potted plants. Mixed with other grades for use in aquariums	.08
5	Large Lumps	For display windows. For outside borders. (Never packed in mesh bags)	

All sizes supplied in bulk being packed in bags of 100 lbs. each.
List price for bulk packing, per lb. $ .05

19

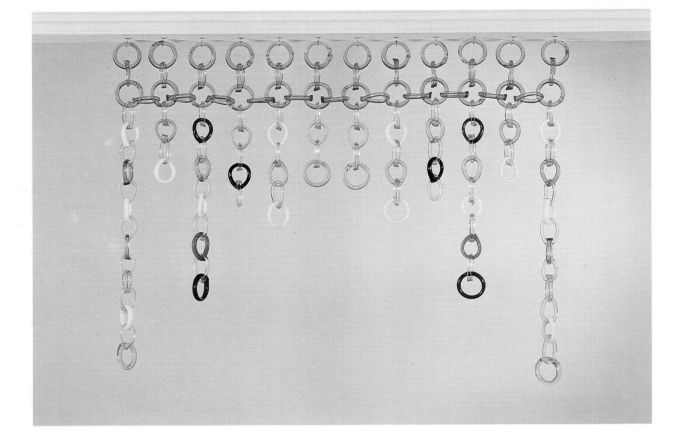

As we exit the story of Akro Agate, it's appropriate we do it via the unusual glass chain doorway shown here. This particular hanging glass chain was made as a special birthday gift for Cora Marsh, a first cousin of Gilbert Marsh, who was a founder of Akro Agate. Look at the colorful Akro colors of each piece of the chain! This one has survived ownership (and use!) of three people, not to mention the journey to be photographed; so it must be a lot sturdier than you'd imagine — or it's had very careful handling, or both! It serves as a kind of tribute to a remarkable glassware known as Akro Agate.